THE GREAT WAR MEMOIR OF RALPH ELLIS,
SUSSEX ARTIST AND SOLDIER

THE GREAT WAR MEMOIR OF RALPH ELLIS, SUSSEX ARTIST AND SOLDIER

EDITED BY SUE HEPBURN

SUSSEX RECORD SOCIETY
VOLUME 100

Issued to members of the Society for 2018/19

Published 2020 by
Sussex Record Society
Barbican House,
High Street,
Lewes,
East Sussex, BN7 1YE.

© Sussex Record Society, Sue Hepburn
ISBN 978 0 85445 082 4

Printed by Hobbs the Printers Ltd., Totton, Hampshire

VOLUMES ISSUED BY THE SUSSEX RECORD SOCIETY

   Vol. 1   Marriage Licences at Lewes, 1586-1642
   Vol. 2   *Sussex Fines, 1190-1248*
   Vol. 3   *Post Mortem Inquisitions, 1558-1583*
   Vol. 4   *Ecclesiastical Returns for East Sussex, 1603; Sussex Poll Book, 1705;*
Sussex MSS in the Harleian MSS; Bishop Praty's Register, 1438-1445.
   Vol. 5   *West Sussex Protestation Returns, 1641-1642*
   Vol. 6   *Marriage Licences at Lewes, 1670-1732*
   Vol. 7   *Sussex Fines, 1249-1307*
   Vol. 8   *Bishop Rede's Register, 1397-1415 (Pt. 1)*
   Vol. 9   *Marriage Licences at Chichester 1575-1730*
   Vol. 10   *Subsidy Rolls, 1296, 1327 and 1332*
   Vol. 11   *Bishop Rede's Register, 1397-1415 (Pt. 2)*
   Vol. 12   *Marriage Licences at Chichester (peculiars), 1579-1730*
   Vol. 13   *Cuckfield Parish Register, 1598-1699*
   Vol. 14   *Post Mortem Inquisitions, 1485-1649*
   Vol. 15   *Bolney Parish Register, 1541-1812*
   Vol. 16   *Star Chamber Proceedings, 1500-1558*
* Vol. 17   *Ardingly Parish Register, 1558-1812*
   Vol. 18   *Angmering Parish Register, 1562-1687*
   Vol. 19   *Sussex Manors and Advowsons, etc., 1509-1833, A-L*
   Vol. 20   *Sussex Manors and Advowsons, etc., 1509-1833, M-Z*
   Vol. 21   *Horsham Parish Register, 1541-1635*
   Vol. 22   *Cowfold Parish Register, 1558-1812*
* Vol. 23   *Sussex Fines, 1308-1509*
   Vol. 24   *East Grinstead Parish Register, 1558-1661*
   Vol. 25   *Marriage Licences at Lewes, 1771-1837, A-L*
   Vol. 26   *Marriage Licences at Lewes, 1772-1837, M-Z*
   Vol. 27   *Preston Manor Court Rolls, 1562-1702*
   Vol. 28   *Sussex Apprentices and Masters, 1710-1752*
   Vol. 29   *Abstracts of Documents relating to the Dobell family, 16th-18th cents.*
   Vol. 30   *Glynde Parish Register, 1558-1812*
   Vol. 31   *Custumals of the Sussex Manors of the Bishop of Chichester, c.1256-1374*
   Vol. 32   *Sussex Marriage Licences at Chichester, 1731-1774*
   Vol. 33   *Sussex Inquisitions (from Bodleian Library), 1541-1616*
   Vol. 34   *The Book of John Rowe, Steward to Lord Bergavenny, 1622*
   Vol. 35   *Marriage Licences at Chichester, 1775-1800, with Index 1731-1800*
   Vol. 36   *Sussex Chantry Records, 1535-1652*
   Vol. 37   *Hastings Rape Records, 1387-1474*
   Vol. 38   *Chartulary of Lewes Priory (Pt. I), 11th-14th cents.*
   Vol. 39   *The Buckhurst Terrier, 1597-1598*

Vol. 40 *Chartulary of Lewes Priory (Pt. II), 12th-14th cents.*
Vol. 41 *Transcripts of Sussex Wills up to 1560 Vol.1 Albourne - Chichester*
Vol. 42 *Transcripts of Sussex Wills up to 1560 Vol.2 Chiddingly - Horsham*
Vol. 43 *Transcripts of Sussex Wills up to 1560 Vol.3 Horsted Keynes - Pyecombe*
Vol. 44 *Records of the Barony and Honour of the Rape of Lewes, 1265-1466*
Vol. 45 *Transcripts of Sussex Wills up to 1560 Vol.4 Racton - Yapton*
Vol. 46 *Chichester Cathedral Chartulary, 13th-16th cents.*
Vol. 47 *Survey of Robertsbridge Manor, 1567-1570*
Vol. 48 *The Town Book of Lewes, 1542-1701*
Vol. 49 *Churchwardens' Presentments, (Pt. I), Archdeaconry of Chichester, 1621-28, 1664-70*
Vol. 50 *Churchwardens' Presentments, (Pt. II), Archdeaconry of Lewes, 1674-1677*
Vol. 51 *Record of Deputations of Gamekeepers, 1781-1928*

Jubilee Volume *Sussex Views from the Burrell Collection*

Vol. 52 *Chapter Acts, Chichester, 1472-1544 (The White Act Book)*
Vol. 53 *The Manor of Etchingham cum Salehurst, 1597-1865*
Vol. 54 *Quarter Sessions Order Book, 1642-1649*
Vol. 55 *Ministers' Accounts of the Manor of Petworth, 1347-1353*
Vol. 56 *Lay Subsidy Rolls, 1524-1525*
Vol. 57 *Custumals of Sussex Manors of the Archbishop of Canterbury, 1285-1330*
Vol. 58 *Chapter Acts, Chichester, 1545-1642*
Vol. 59 *Chartulary of Boxgrove Priory, 12th-14th cents.*
Vol. 60 *Custumals of the Manors of Laughton, Willingdon and Goring, 1292-1338*
Vol. 61 *A Catalogue of Sussex Estate and Tithe Award Maps (Pt. 1), 1606-1884*
Vol. 62 *Minutes of the Common Council of the City of Chichester, 1783-1826*
Vol. 63 *The Book of Bartholomew Bolney, 15th cent.*
Vol. 64 *Rye Shipping Records, 1566-1590*
Vol. 65 *Cellarers' Rolls of Battle Abbey, 1275-1513*
Vol. 66 *A Catalogue of Sussex Maps, (Pt. II) 1597-1958*
Vol. 67 *Estate Surveys of the Fitzalan Earls of Arundel, 14th cent.*
Vol. 68 *The Journal of Giles Moore of Horsted Keynes, 1655-1679*
Vol. 69 *The Town Book of Lewes, 1702-1837*
Vol. 70 *The Town Book of Lewes, 1837-1901*
Vol. 71 *Accounts of the Roberts Family of Boarzell, 1568-1582*
Vol. 72 *Printed Maps of Sussex, 1575-1900*
Vol. 73 *Correspondence of the Dukes of Richmond and Newcastle, 1724-1750*
Vol. 74 *Sussex Coroners' Inquests, 1485-1558*
Vol. 75 *The Religious Census of Sussex, 1851*
Vol. 76 *The Fuller Letters, 1728-1755*
Vol. 77 *East Sussex Land Tax, 1785*

* Vol. 78 *Chichester Diocesan Surveys, 1686 and 1724*
* Vol. 79 *Saint Richard of Chichester*
  Vol. 80 *The Ashdown Forest Dispute, 1876-1882*
  Vol. 81 *Sussex Schools in the 18th century*
  Vol. 82 *West Sussex Land Tax, 1785*
  Vol. 83 *Mid Sussex Poor Law Records, 1601-1835*
  Vol. 84 *Sussex in the First World War*
  Vol. 85 *Sussex Depicted: Views and Descriptions 1600-1800*
  Vol. 86 *Sussex Shore to Flanders Fields: E. Heron–Allen's Journal of the Great War*
* Vol. 87 *East Sussex Parliamentary Deposited Plans, 1799-1970*
  Vol. 88 *Sussex Cricket in the 18th century*
  Vol. 89 *East Sussex Coroners' Records, 1688-1838*
  Vol. 90 *The Durford Cartulary*
* Vol. 91 *Sussex Clergy Inventories, 1600-1750*
* Vol. 92 *Accounts and Records of the Manor of Mote in Iden, 1461-1551, 1673*
* Vol. 93 *East Sussex Church Monuments, 1530-1830*
* Vol. 94 *Winchelsea Poor Law Records, 1790-1841*
* Vol. 95 *Littlehampton School Logbook, 1871-1911*
* Vol. 96 *Letters of John Collier of Hastings, 1731-1746*
* Vol. 97 *Chichester Archdeaconry Depositions, 1603-1608*
* Vol. 98 *Church Surveys of Chichester Archdeaconry, 1602, 1610 & 1636*
* Vol. 99 *Facing Invasion: Proceedings Under the Defence Acts 1801-05*

In print volumes marked with an asterisk can be obtained from the Sussex Record Society, Barbican House, Lewes, East Sussex, BN7 1YE or through the Society's website: www.sussexrecordsociety.org

CONTENTS

Acknowledgements	xi
List of Additional Illustrations	xiii
Introduction	1
Life before the war	11
Volume I	13
Volume II	33
Volume III	71
Volume IV	117
Volume V	181
Life after the war	249
Appendix: Letters from the front	255
Bibliography	277
Index	279

ACKNOWLEDGEMENTS

A century after it was written the Great War memoir of Ralph Ellis is at last available to the wider audience it so richly deserves. This would not have been possible without the invaluable contribution of all those who have been involved with the publication, to whom I am indebted.

First and foremost, I offer my thanks to Ralph Ellis, artist, writer, designer, volunteer soldier and man of Sussex, without whom this volume would not exist. He wrote and painted a personal story that speaks not only for himself, but also for his comrades in the 7th Battalion, Royal Sussex Regiment and all those who served in the infantry in the Great War. It has been an honour and a pleasure to work on this extraordinary document.

Ralph's daughter, Margaret Gowler, who sadly passed away before seeing the published volume, was generous both with her time and her memories of her father. I am grateful to her for allowing me to draw freely on her excellent biography of her father, which tells so much about his life before and after the Great War and gives a sense of the person behind the pictures and words.

I would like to thank Wendy Walker and all the staff at the West Sussex Record Office, where Ralph's memoir and related material are safely preserved for posterity within the wider context of the Royal Sussex Regimental Archive. In particular my thanks go to Wendy, Martin Hayes, Claire Snoad and Jennifer Mason for all their support and for helping to make this project a reality.

As the hundredth volume issued by the Sussex Record Society, this edition takes its place among the wealth of historical material from the county of Sussex now available to the public. I am very grateful to the Council of the Society for publishing the volume, and particularly to Peter Wilkinson and Danae Tankard for their assistance, and Brian Short for his support, past and present. Roger Pearce has produced a stunning design that perfectly complements the memoir and displays additional material to perfection. My thanks also go to Roger for his advice, patience and attention to detail, all of which have been invaluable.

Jane Lenaghan and Alan Readman read early drafts of my commentary, and with their combined knowledge of the Great War and the Royal Sussex Regiment they were able to provide me with numerous helpful comments and suggestions, for which I am most grateful.

Arundel Museum is the repository for a collection of material pertaining to Ralph Ellis, and thanks are due to Fran Stovold and Malcolm Farquharson for their assistance in making the material available and allowing it to be reproduced in this volume. I am also grateful to Eric Nash, who may know more about Arundel than anyone else alive, for sharing his personal knowledge of Ralph and for allowing me to use his own material to enrich this book. Thanks to the National Archives, Ralph's Officer Service Record is publicly available, as is his registration record for the Slade School of Art, and I am grateful for their permission to use the material here.

Finally, I would like to thank my husband, John Godfrey, for introducing me to Ralph Ellis nearly twenty years ago and for sharing my passion for the Great War.

Sue Hepburn, December 2019

DEDICATION

This volume is dedicated to all the men of the 7th Battalion, Royal Sussex Regiment who fought in the Great War 1914 to 1918.

LIST OF ADDITIONAL ILLUSTRATIONS

William "Benner" Ellis outside his premises at 12 High Street Arundel (ARUHC: P00381 courtesy of Arundel Museum Society) 11
Marriage of Ralph Ellis and Gertrude Seymour (Photo 12) 12
A Call to Arms, 7th Battalion recruitment poster (WSRO, RSR/MSS/7/5) 13
7th Battalion Royal Sussex Regiment at Chichester Station (WSRO, RSR/PH/16/15) 14
Front cover, Memoir Vol 1 (WSRO Add MS 25002) 17
Ralph Ellis: Self-Portrait (ARUHC:01738.1992 courtesy of Arundel Museum Society) 74
Ralph Ellis in the uniform of 2nd Lieut, The Queen's (Royal West Surrey) Regiment (WSRO Add MS 25001) 185
Rear cover, Memoir Vol 5 (WSRO Add MS 25006 65) 248
Ralph Ellis: Arundel View (ARUHC:02452.2000 courtesy of Arundel Museum Society) 249
Ralph and Gertrude Ellis (WSRO, Acc 19236) 250
Ralph Ellis: The Railway Tavern pub sign (WSRO, PH 16225/38) 251
Ralph Ellis: Landscape painting of a downland view 1954 (ARUHC:03260.2020 courtesy of Arundel Museum Society) 252
Ralph Ellis at his Easel (WSRO, Acc 19236) 253

INTRODUCTION

The Great War memoir of Ralph Ellis is a Sussex gem. In paintings, drawings and words it tells the story of the men of the 7th Battalion, Royal Sussex Regiment between the outbreak of war in August 1914 and December 1916 when the author left the Battalion to train for a commission. A Sussex man himself, Ralph was born and grew up in Arundel and after a period away returned in the early 1920s, living there for the rest of his life. He served with the county regiment, which had links with Sussex from the early nineteenth century, formally becoming the county regiment in 1881. The majority of Ralph's comrades were also Sussex men, certainly during the early volunteer recruitment period, although it changed after conscription was introduced in 1916. With the Royal Sussex Regimental archive and collection, along with Ralph's memoir, now residing at West Sussex Record Office, and with the interest generated by the commemorations of the centenary of the Great War, this is the perfect time for Ralph's remarkable testimony to be available to a wider audience.

By the outbreak of war Ralph was becoming established as an artist and throughout his time in the army he made sketches and watercolours of what he saw, these images becoming the basis of his memoir. He made notes and wrote letters, which he also used as sources, posting the material home to his wife and family for safekeeping. The memoir was written in five large manuscript volumes, the first of which was started while Ralph was on leave in 1916. He continued to write it during the latter part of the fifteen months he spent in hospitals in 1917 and 1918 and completed the fifth volume in 1921.[1, 2]

The first volume mainly comprises pencil sketches of fellow recruits captured at moments of rest during the period of training and also a few civilians in billets or organising recreational activities. The brief text describes the initial training period before embarking for France.[3] In Book II the focus shifts to pencil sketches of landscapes, shelled towns, villages and houses observed on arrival in France. There are also some drawings of trenches, dugouts, billets and field kitchens showing the more domestic side of life at the Front, as well as some of Ralph's comrades at rest. Here much of the text is either in the form of long captions accompanying the pictures or has been inserted afterwards, giving the impression of a series of episodes rather than a continuous narrative.[4] These first two volumes resemble scrapbooks of visual and written impressions and are portrait in aspect. Books III, IV and V are more organised, with pencil sketches and watercolours of countryside, towns and villages, and buildings both scarred and untouched by war, alternating with pages of text written in

---

[1] The five volumes of Ralph's memoirs are unpaginated; I have inserted page numbers here as a guide.
[2] WSRO Add. Mss. 25001: 152; WSRO Add. Mss. 25006: 235.
[3] WSRO Add. Mss. 25002.
[4] WSRO Add. Mss. 25003.

Ralph's elegant script, forming a loosely chronological narrative.[5] With these three volumes, the aspect changes to landscape.

The value of Ralph's images is that they depict the everyday life of a soldier on the Western Front. They show what he saw and believed to be worth recording. Although photography was becoming more popular at the time of the Great War, particularly among officers, for security reasons it was discouraged and later restricted to official photographers. Few men serving in the ranks had access to a camera so Ralph's talents with pencil and brush were valuable commodities. It was no coincidence that he was deployed as an observer, directing artillery, machine gun and sniper fire. With his artist's eye for details in the landscape, and operating from a vantage point with a good view of the battlefield, he was able to spot where the enemy was operating, quickly record the information and direct British fire accordingly. Sketches he made from 'O. Pips' or observation posts give a unique perspective on trench warfare, illustrating the landscape from behind British lines across no man's land to the German trenches. This was a view rarely seen by infantrymen in the trenches – unless they were going over the top in an offensive – as looking over the parapet resulted in almost certain injury or death.[6]

Although Ralph started his memoir by collecting his sketches together and adding some text to complement the images, as it evolved the balance shifted and the narrative became more prominent. When he revised his memoir in 1947-1948 the original manuscripts were edited into one volume, typewritten and bound into book form, entitled *A March with the Infantry,* but with no sketches or watercolours included. This was a conscious decision on Ralph's part as he says in a brief introduction,

> [The] sketches, which do not include the more interesting and dramatic subjects seen when one had no time for using the pencil, were made when the opportunity occurred; therefore were they useless as a means of conveying any idea of the life of the Infantry, without an attempt to place by their side words conveying the impressions that remained most vivid in the memory.[7]

Despite Ralph's artistic talent, he felt the images he created did not fully express his most vivid memories and he needed to use words to give them meaning. As he says, this was partly due to the limited opportunities available for drawing and painting while engaged in military duties, particularly when in front line trenches. Although he drew some shell-damaged buildings and blasted woods, many of his landscapes show little evidence of war. When he includes the dead they are portrayed as shapeless bundles and are unrecognisable, or they are represented by crosses in a cemetery. Soldiers are rarely depicted in the landscape and if they are, they are shown digging or

[5] WSRO Add. Mss. 25004-6.
[6] WSRO Add. Mss. 25005: 111.
[7] WSRO Add. Mss. 25001: 2.

hauling rather than fighting or killing. His trenches are empty; his combatants are resting in billets. However, this is not the war that Ralph portrays in his writing. In his narrative the dead are close-by and encountered often on sorties to mend the barbed wire entanglements in no man's land. Although he acknowledges they have 'done their work and greatly', the horror and fear of death is expressed vividly:

> There seems to be a portion of a body in almost every shell hole… on finding oneself bending low over a misshapen, evil smelling form, they possess this dark, sodden soil, limbs grotesque and vague meet you frequently sticking out from the soft earth…[8]

There is evidently a tension between the written and the visual representation of Ralph's experience of war. Perhaps he lacked the artistic language necessary to convey his impressions through a visual medium. Unlike the Great War 'war artists', many of whom adopted the anti-naturalistic conventions of Modernism to portray the devastation they saw, Ralph adhered to the English landscape tradition and struggled to convey the anti-landscape and 'annihilation of Nature' produced by war.[9] He may have used his art subconsciously as an escape from the realities of war and to try to counteract the destruction he saw around him.

As the memoir developed, Ralph increasingly used words to complement his images and to convey the details of his experiences. The narrative, which tells of the movements of the Battalion from their arrival in France in June 1915 until December 1916 when Ralph gained a commission, forms a thread that links a series of impressions and incidents. While it is broadly chronological, at times Ralph's ordering of events does not follow exactly the movements of his unit as recorded in the War Diary of the 7th Battalion, Royal Sussex Regiment.[10]

As an artist, Ralph's talent is to be able to translate the detail he observed into images. As a writer he does something similar and, in effect, paints pictures with words. As well as describing what he saw in detail, including billets, ruined buildings, landscapes and wildlife, he also relates his experiences, including wiring parties, exploding mines and difficult reliefs. The vocabulary is plain and naturalistic, aiming for realism, with none of the 'big words' and 'high abstractions' often associated with Great War writing. According to Samuel Hynes, by 1915 the notions of Honour, Glory, Valour and Sacrifice promoted by poets like Rupert Brooke were being rejected by some who were in the midst of the action on the Western Front. In a letter to his fiancée, Vera Brittain,

---

[8] WSRO Add. Mss. 25005: 126.
[9] Hynes (1990): 196; see also Paul Nash, 'The Menin Road' and 'We are making a new world' (Imperial War Museum), CRW Nevinson, 'La Mitrailleuse'(Imperial War Museum) and 'Returning to the Trenches' (Metropolitan Museum of Art).
[10] WSRO RSR/MSS/7/11.

the soldier-poet Roland Leighton articulated his antipathy to the use of chivalric language and abstract values and promoted the use of realism.[11]

Ralph focuses on the physical, he is concerned with sensations, with sight, sound, smell and touch, as shown in the following extract:

> We pass on over the sheltering ridge and the road becomes a part of the other shelled ground, its surface churned into a thick mass which tires the feet, partially fills the shell hole and covers the dead mules. The darkness hides much, but in such a place that intense nauseating smell, combination of fumes from H. E. shells and rotting flesh – the odour of blood and iron. This is sufficient to direct one to the Front.
>
> The last of our heavies is past, head down, slogging along that foul track, the wall of blackness on our left is ripped is suddenly split open discharging a volume of noise and flame so near that for a second our eyes are blinded by the violent intensity of the flash and the senses are numbed by the force of the discharge. The momentary impression is that a shell has burst right in our midst. The Platoon wakes up, sort of feels round to find out if one is still whole, curses the gunners, laughs and settles down once more to the dogged endurance of the march.[12]

This passage, which describes his platoon marching to the front-line trenches to relieve another battalion, encapsulates the desire to report the experience of war 'as it was' both through the senses and through emotions: the fear, exhaustion, resignation and humour. Hynes states that this descriptive, realistic, physical style is typical of Great War memoirs, particularly those written with no literary pretensions by 'one-book amateurs'.[13]

Throughout his life Ralph drew and painted the landscape, particularly the Sussex countryside around his home in Arundel. Many of his fellow servicemen shared his love of Sussex scenery and John Godfrey argues that an attachment to the landscapes of Sussex (and in particular the chalk landscapes of the South Downs) motivated and sustained Sussex men fighting for their county and country.[14] While serving in France Ralph used his free time, when the battalion was in rest, to sketch and paint the French countryside, incorporating many examples in his memoir.

The memoir also contains many written passages celebrating the beauty of the countryside, particularly when contrasted with the devastation of war. Having been in the line throughout the brutal winter of 1915 to 1916, the 'radiant glory' Ralph

---

[11] Hynes (1990): 112.
[12] WSRO Add. Mss. 25006: 183-185.
[13] Hynes (1997): 26-7.
[14] Godfrey [n.d.].

experienced when marching into rest behind the lines in the spring of 1916 was overwhelming. Whereas the front line was a 'winter of desolation', the French countryside was 'a pulsating host of minute things gently but surely being brought into life.' It was the life force of nature that inspired him and gave him hope, the thousands of mating birds, flowers and insects, compared with the death and devastation he had witnessed at the front.[15]

For many Sussex men, in July 1916 the open chalk landscapes of the Somme region bore a striking resemblance to the South Downs. Returning to the Somme battlefield in the autumn of 1916, Ralph was deeply shocked by the destruction of this once-familiar landscape by three months of intense fighting. The 'dead brown land' had been fought over 'foot by foot' with a 'scorching flame, licking the earth to brown ashes, striking down every tree… turning a fair land into stark desolation'. He lamented the destruction caused by the war and it depressed him 'to think that all our progress must be made at such a cost'.[16]

When writing about the countryside and nature Ralph's language changes and his style becomes lyrical, romantic and poetic, employing literary devices to enrich his descriptions. Returning to the Somme region twelve months later he witnessed a transformation:

> …nature had leapt back to her tortured, naked earth with all the abandoned love and sympathy of a mother. Shell holes and trenches were entirely hidden beneath a prolific growth of green grasses… a setting for every specie [sic] of wild flower this land knew… great masses of small white flowers heaped together like a bridal wreath… Then nature clapped her hands, laughed and the scheme changed, tall yellow flowers gained the day, ran riot over the hummocks, bent to the light breeze and shook their golden heads in the sunlight…[17]

Ralph's pleasure in the regeneration of the countryside is expressed in the richness of the imagery, which adds vivacity and energy to the picture. Here 'Nature' is personified and given human emotions and actions; she is reminiscent of the classical goddess of nature, which alludes to the ancient and enduring quality of nature. The passage is particularly striking as it is juxtaposed with descriptions of the mutilation of not only the landscape, but also of the equipment, horses and men who were negotiating the devastated countryside in order to reach the Front.

Despite Ralph's joy, he cannot forget the price paid by the men who lost their lives, whose spilt blood is represented by poppies.

---

[15] WSRO Add. Mss. 25005: 137.
[16] WSRO Add. Mss. 25006: 187.
[17] Ibid: 189.

> Then as though she had remembered suddenly how all this land had been bought, came laden with deep red poppies, massed together and in rivulets of red, and let them dribble out into the green they flowed out into the green, like the blood that had been so freely spilt here. Over all these flowers, dancing in the sunlight were many butterflies...[18]

Paul Fussell argues that the poppy is inseparable from Great War writings, symbolising among other things, eternal sleep, death and remembrance. Ralph would have been aware of these literary references, which are found for example in one of the most popular poems of the war, John McCrae's 'In Flanders Fields'.[19] Many species of butterflies proliferated among the flowers recalling English country gardens, but also representing life after death.[20]

If Ralph was searching for a source of comfort to sustain him during the darkest days of the war, surely he found it in the power of nature. On different occasions he attributes the transformation of living things to a higher being: 'the God who gave them life', 'a master gardener' and Mother Nature. Conversely, the destruction was due to the actions of men, who created a 'God-forsaken country, burnt bare of life.'[21]

According to his daughter, Ralph was a spiritual man and in later life he attended church regularly. The memoir provides glimpses of his beliefs, but he rarely writes overtly about religion. He regards war as a 'lottery' and for Ralph perhaps the best philosophy for a fighting soldier was to live in the moment and not worry about what lay in the past or the future. When marching towards the Somme in the summer of 1916 he says 'Fate was their God, and decided whether they must live or die'.[22]

Throughout the memoir Ralph shows enormous admiration and respect for the men with whom he served. Many of his sketches are of his comrades, both in individual portraits and collectively engaged in a variety of activities. In his narrative he writes affectionately of their courage, their stoicism and their humour, which helped to sustain them all. The high regard in which he held his comrades is emphasised in a short passage in Volume V, at the point when he leaves the 7th Royal Sussex to take up his commission. He pays tribute to the 'original 1100 men drawn by the spirit of high adventure and patriotism', of whom 'few remain' and remembers the 'pluck' of those who died, were disabled and those who soldier on.

> The Battalion marches on and its ranks are filled by other men who knew it not in its younger days of inspiration and comradeship, but they carry on through many of the differing phases of the war, finally reaping the results of the work of

---

[18] Ibid.
[19] Fussell (2000): 246-7.
[20] Lewis-Stempel (2006): 200.
[21] WSRO Add. Mss. 25006: 187, 189.
[22] WSRO Add. Mss. 25005: 150.

men who also suffered, laughed and fought through the long tedious days of the first 3 years of war.[23]

His acknowledgement of the vital contribution made by these men to the war effort suggests his possible motivation for writing the memoir – as a memorial to his comrades. While being intensely personal, it was a shared experience; he rarely wrote in the first person singular, 'I', but usually in the first person plural, 'we' – emphasising that they were all in it together.

As well as creating a memorial to the men he served with in the 7th Royal Sussex, Ralph was also, consciously or not, making sense of the extraordinary events he had experienced and attempting to cope with the trauma he had suffered; it was a form of catharsis. Hynes argues that war narratives are responses to a 'primal need', present in everyone, to tell and to hear individual stories in order to understand our own lives and imagine the lives of others.[24] Like many who fought he may have felt guilty for surviving when so many of his comrades died. On at least two occasions, when on leave in March 1916 and again at the beginning of July 1916 when he was at Divisional HQ at Henencourt, he missed actions when the Battalion was involved in heavy fighting with many casualties.[25] He obviously felt this keenly as he mentions both occasions in Volume IV and also in his revised memoir, *A March with the Infantry*.[26]

Thanks to the introduction of compulsory elementary education in 1870, the majority of men who went to war in 1914-18 were literate and as a result many Great War testimonies have survived. Officers and men in the ranks from across the Royal Sussex Regiment have left records of their experiences, from brief notes and letters to loved ones to detailed journals or diaries and published autobiographies.

As well as Ralph's memoir, there are other surviving testimonies from the 7th Battalion.[27] A number of employees from the Shippams Factory in Chichester enlisted in August 1914 and served together in the 7th Royal Sussex. Many of them, including George Farndale and Charles Tulett, corresponded regularly with the managing director of the company, Ernest Shippam, to keep him updated about their progress and to stay in touch with news from the factory, where they expected to return after the war. Their letters, with others written by Shippams employees, are in the West Sussex Record Office, along with an unpublished memoir written by Charles Tulett.[28] Letters home also form the basis of the testimony of Alfred Sansom, who became commanding officer of the 7th Battalion in October 1916, having previously served in the 5th Battalion. Throughout his time in France he wrote every day to his wife, Ivy, in Bexhill, with

---

[23] WSRO Add. Mss. 25006: 209.
[24] Hynes (1997): 16.
[25] WSRO Add. Mss. 25001: 102.
[26] WSRO Add. Mss. 25005: 128-131; introduction to Vol. IV.
[27] Godfrey [n.d.].
[28] WSRO Add. Mss. 1606; WSRO RSR uncatalogued (Museum Accession 3179).

detailed accounts of his activities. After his death in July 1917, Ivy edited the letters and had a 380-page volume printed, entitled *Letters from France*.[29] Ivan Margary, also an officer with the 7th Battalion from June 1916 until he was demobilised in 1919, wrote an account of his wartime experiences, which is in the library of the Sussex Archaeological Society in Lewes, East Sussex.[30]

It is, however, the (sometimes fictionalised) autobiographies that are best remembered and that have influenced perceptions of the Great War. One of the most respected of these, *Undertones of War*, was written by Edmund Blunden, who fought in the 11th Battalion, Royal Sussex Regiment. Others include *Memoirs of an Infantry Officer* by Siegfried Sassoon and *Goodbye to All That* by Robert Graves. They were written by public school educated men who served as officers and who were established or aspiring literary figures. Published a decade or so after the war ended, the memoirs were always intended for wider audience, presenting a particular perspective that has shaped the way the war is now understood.[31] The act of consciously writing a personal account for publication can have an impact on the way it is written, the material selected and omitted and the version of the self the author chooses to promote.

There is nothing to suggest that publication was the motive when Ralph's testimony was first compiled and written. Even when he edited his memoir into a continuous narrative in 1947-48, in the main leaving the text as it was in the original, the typewritten copy that exists in the WSRO appears to be the only one printed and there is no evidence he ever intended it to be published. Rather than crediting himself as the author he uses his anonymous service number of Four-Two-Eight, perhaps to emphasise that his experience was a common one and could represent all the infantrymen who he had served with, many of whom died. However, in 1956 he loaned the original five manuscript volumes to the Royal Sussex Regimental Museum at Chichester Barracks, where he had enlisted forty-two years previously. Perhaps he wanted to make his testimony accessible to a wider audience and to ensure they survived for posterity.

Although Ralph was later promoted to a temporary commission, he only served as an officer for a short time before being wounded. In his memoir he focuses on his service in the ranks of the 7th Royal Sussex, which was his defining experience, making it of particular value as it provides an alternative viewpoint. While junior officers served in the trenches alongside the men, and were not safely ensconced some miles to the rear

---

[29] Sansom (1921).
[30] Margary [n.d.].
[31] What Samuel Hynes has called 'The Myth of the Great War': [A] generation of innocent young men, their heads full of high abstractions like Honour, Glory and England, went off to war to make the world safe for democracy. They were slaughtered in stupid battles planned by stupid generals. Those who survived were shocked, disillusioned and embittered by their war experiences, and saw that their real enemies were not the Germans, but the old men at home who had lied to them. They rejected the values of the society that had sent them to war, and in doing so separated their own generation from the past and from their cultural inheritance. Hynes (1990): p. x.

as some representations may suggest, a particular power relationship existed meaning they were set apart and enjoyed certain privileges. This was not the case for Ralph, who as an NCO lived and worked among the men, whom he counted as his comrades.

Unlike the published memoirs there is no criticism of the way the war was being conducted, or any sense of him being against the war. Like the vast majority of servicemen he believed there was a job to be done and he had to do it. The only hint of disapproval was his despair at the senseless waste, cruelty and destruction of war. In a letter home to his mother in September 1916, written after a spell fighting on the front line at the Somme, he deplores the 'frightfulness' of war, suggesting that if man can 'make such an unspeakable hell of things' it is time to put 'as much effort into making life the very opposite to this'. However, at the same time he affirms his belief that people of 'any nationality are alright, or much the same in their knowledge of good and evil'. A 'great leader' is needed to lead countries 'up out of these animal hates'.[32]

Written during and immediately after the war, Ralph's account has the advantage of immediacy. Issues concerning the reliability of memory must always be considered when approaching a personal testimony as historical evidence; memory is subjective and every individual present at an event will have a personal interpretation. With the passage of time memories can become confused and there are instances in Ralph's narrative where the timing of events is muddled and out of order when compared to the official record, something he attempted to address in his 1940s edition. The memoir is a genuine attempt by an ordinary man to portray the extraordinary circumstances he encountered as an infantryman on the Western Front.

It is also worth remembering that for the men fighting on the ground events were often confusing and disorientating; they were unable to see the bigger picture. At the time offensives did not have specific names, they were known by generic terms such as the 'Big Push'. It was only after the war, in 1920, that the Battles Nomenclature Committee at the War Office gave names to the various actions and continuous narratives were constructed.[33]

Whilst the power of the memoir lies in its personal perspective, it cannot tell the whole story. With limited information about the chronology and the movements of the battalion, it is necessary to set the memoir within the context of the official records. The original War Diary of the 7th Battalion, Royal Sussex Regiment is held in the Royal Sussex Regimental archive at West Sussex Record Office and is available to view online.[34] This records the details of the daily movements and activities of the battalion from 1915 to 1919. By outlining the whereabouts of the 7th Battalion in the introduction to each of the volumes of the memoir, a context is provided for the narrative, enabling

[32] Letter to mother, 12 September 1916 Appendix: 271.
[33] TNA WO161/102.
[34] WSRO RSR/MSS/7/11

the reader to connect the two sources and enrich one with the other. A further useful source is the official history of the 7th Battalion, Royal Sussex Regiment during the Great War. Published in the mid 1930s it draws on the surviving official sources and on the testimony of officers and men, one of whom is Ralph Ellis.[35]

The Great War was only four years out of a life of 78 years and it is important to set Ralph's wartime experiences within the context of a long life, lived mainly in Sussex. Although the focus of this book is his wartime memoir, it also includes information about his childhood and his post-war years, both spent in his home town of Arundel. Like many disabled veterans who returned home, he had to cope with his physical and mental injuries and get on with his life, with little support outside his immediate family and community. Ralph's artistic talents helped him to build a new life as a designer and painter of inn signs and a landscape artist, gaining a considerable reputation in both fields and earning a blue plaque on the family home in Maltravers Street, Arundel in 1995. The source document for these periods of his life is an unpublished biography written by his daughter, Margaret Gowler. Making use of Ralph's business records she gives a detailed account of his professional work over some forty years as well as telling the more personal story of his family life. The biography also contains transcripts of some of the letters written by Ralph to his parents and sisters from the Western Front, which are reproduced in Appendix A.[36]

On October 21st 1915 the following item appeared in the West Sussex Gazette:

> 'We have seen with much interest many sketches sent home from France to his wife by Sergeant R. G. Ellis, of the 7th Batt. Royal Sussex... They portray scenes in and about the trenches... the scenery of war and glimpses of the gallant fellows who are maintaining the honour of the old country in most stressful circumstances. Some of the sketches would certainly repay reproduction.'[37]

Over a hundred years later Ralph's pictures and words are being reproduced in this publication. It is a fitting memorial to all those who fought in the Great War 1914 to 1918 and particularly to those Sussex men who fought alongside Ralph in the 7th Battalion, Royal Sussex Regiment.

---

[35] Rutter [n.d.]: 5.
[36] Gowler (1997).
[37] *West Sussex Gazette*, 21 Oct 1915, p. 4.

William "Benner" Ellis outside his premises at 12 High Street Arundel

LIFE BEFORE THE WAR

Ralph Ellis was born on 31st January 1885 in Arundel, West Sussex, a little town of roughly 3,000 inhabitants situated on the River Arun about three miles from the coast. His parents, William and Jane, were married in 1873 and had seven children, of whom Ralph was the youngest. Only four of the siblings were to survive to adulthood; Catherine died aged three years in 1884, before Ralph was born, and two of his brothers, fifteen year old Frederick and Sam, aged eleven, died of typhoid fever in November and December 1890. The source of the epidemic was discovered to be the town pump, which stood in the High Street, and had become contaminated by sewage. The worst-affected families were those living in The Square, who drew their water from the pump. Ralph's father, William, and his thirteen-year-old brother, Jack, also contracted typhoid, but survived. So, the Ellis family was reduced to four children: Emma (born in 1874), Jack (born in 1877), Edith (born in 1882) and Ralph.[38]

The family lived over the shop at 12 High Street, where William was in business as a stationer, interior decorator and taxidermist, the property being rented from the Duke of Norfolk. As well as stuffing and mounting birds and animals for his customers, William also acquired dead kittens, frogs and birds, which he stuffed, mounted and dressed to look like humans in particular scenarios, for example, shops and drawing rooms. These display cases were popular at the time. William was also a keen naturalist and kept a diary of the rare birds and animals that visited Arundel between 1876 and 1925. However, as it seems most of the specimens listed were shot, perhaps William had a professional interest in his hobby.

When he was five Ralph attended the Church of England School in Arundel and later he moved to Mr Toy's Private School in Littlehampton. With a group of Arundel children, he walked to and from the school six days a week in all weathers. In a letter to the West Sussex Gazette in April 1960 Ralph reminisced that the walk on 'the footpath across the meadows from near Arundel Station to Lyminster… gave us a lot of pleasure'. He went on to recall that the journey was not always without incident as 'The boys of Wick took a great dislike to us passing through their territory'.[39]

On leaving school at fourteen, Ralph went to London to join his brother Jack as an apprentice to a furniture designer. But he decided this career was not for him and instead took up interior decoration and sign writing, living in a lodging house in New Barnet. In March 1910 he married Gertrude Ada Seymour, who was from Bognor Regis. The wedding is described in the Bognor Observer on 16th March:

> 'The wedding took place in the Wesleyan Chapel, filled to capacity… The bride was prettily gowned in a dress of white silk eclienne with pearl trimmings and

---

[38] Information about Ralph's early life taken from Gowler (1997): 6-23; Gowler and Leslie (1995); PRO WO 339/83413.
[39] *West Sussex Gazette*, 14 April 1960; quoted in Gowler (1997): 13.

wore a veil and wreath of orange blossoms. She carried a magnificent shower bouquet of tiger lilies, carnations, roses and lilies of the valley.'[40]

Gertrude's sister, Millicent and Ralph's sister, Edith, were bridesmaids.

After they were married the couple lived in New Barnet for about three years and then they moved to Bognor where Ralph opened a little shop in London Road selling home decorating materials and artists' supplies, as well as his own paintings.

When war broke out in August 1914 Ralph volunteered for the army and Gertrude took over the running of the shop.

L-R: Edith Ellis, sister to Ralph; Ralph Ellis; Gertrude Ada Seymour; Best Man; Amelia Seymour, sister to Gertrude

---

[40] *Bognor Observer*, 16 March 1910; quoted in Gowler (1997): 22.

VOLUME 1

Private Ralph Gordon Ellis, number 428, 'C' Company, 9 Platoon, was sworn in and fitted out at Chichester Barracks on 30th August 1914 along with the other recruits in the 7th (Service) Battalion, the Royal Sussex Regiment, the first new battalion of the Royal Sussex Regiment in Kitchener's New Army.

Reasons for volunteering varied with each individual, but patriotism, duty and adventure were high on the list. At the end of his memoir, in a passage dedicated to the men of the 7th Royal Sussex, Ralph says the 'original 1100 men [were] drawn together by the spirit of high adventure and patriotism'.[41]

At nearly thirty years old (the upper age limit for this wave of recruitment), Ralph was not in the first flush of youthful impetuosity, and he had a wife to consider; yet he still decided to join up even though there was no compulsion. The date of his enlistment, 30th August, is significant. On 26th August the *Bognor Regis Observer* printed an appeal by Major Osborne of the Royal Sussex Regiment for 'Sussex men to come forward without delay' to join the 7th Battalion.[42] A week later the paper reported a surge in recruitment at Chichester, especially on 31st August, when the recruiting authorities had 'the busiest day of their lives'.

Kitchener's famous call to arms (Your Country Needs You!), alongside intensive local recruitment campaigns, did their job in persuading the men of Sussex to enlist. By 4th September the 7th Battalion was full and it was decided to form an 8th and 9th Battalion.[43] This enthusiasm was echoed in the national recruiting returns for the week 30th August to 5th September, which were the highest for the whole of the war.[44] According to the History of the Seventh (Service) Battalion, except for a group of about thirty men from Newcastle and Sunderland, the battalion was made up almost entirely of men from Sussex.[45]

A further possible factor for Ralph's volunteering may have been encouragement from his father's landlord, the Duke of Norfolk, who as Lord Lieutenant added his weight to the appeal alongside other members of the aristocracy and gentry. Ralph's older brother, Jack also enlisted early in the war.

Volume I of Ralph's memoir begins as he enlists in August 1914 and follows the movements of the battalion through training and their journey to France at the end of May 1915. The manuscript comprises pencil sketches, many with a short caption, mainly of fellow recruits captured during the period of training. While many of the

---

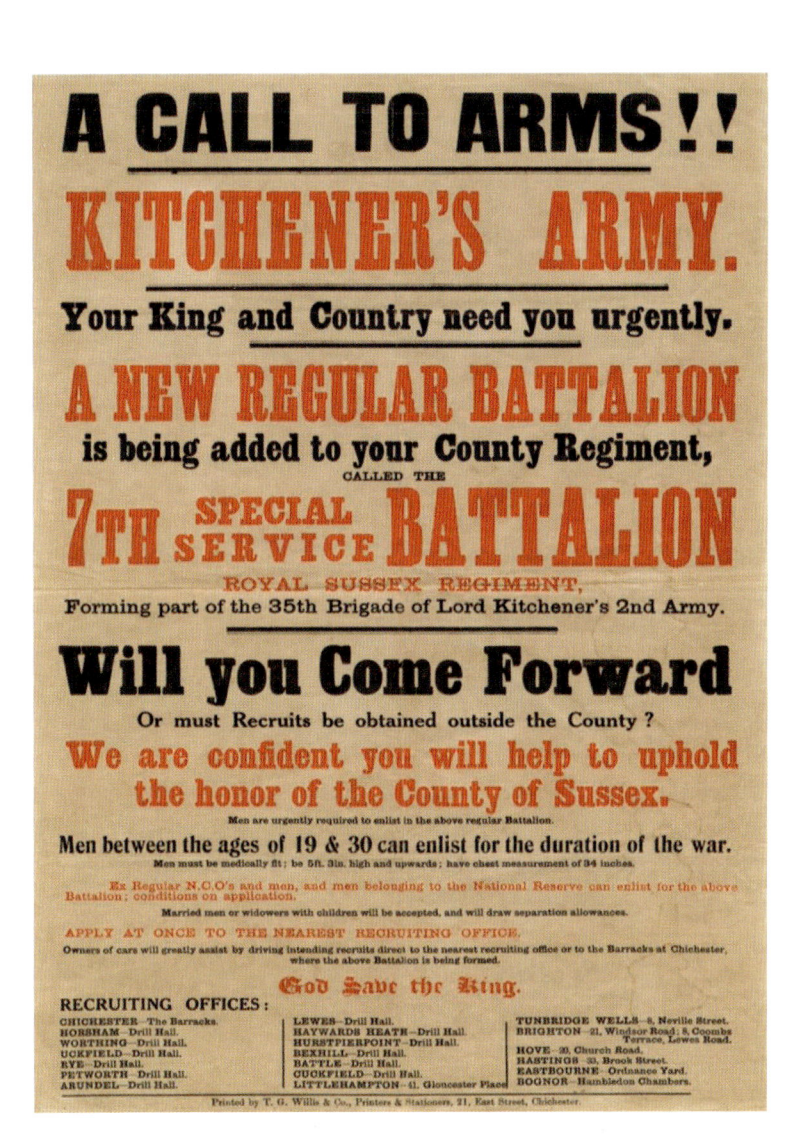

[41] WSRO Add. Mss. 25006: 209.
[42] *Bognor Regis Observer*, 26 August 1914.
[43] Godfrey (2014): 31.
[44] Simkins (1988): 64-5.
[45] Rutter [n.d.]: 5.

7th Battalion RSR at Chichester Station

sketches portray the men at rest – in a recreation room or club – some show them undertaking training activities, for example, on a range-finding course, or performing domestic chores, like shaving. Ralph also sketched some of the civilians he encountered either in billets, selling refreshments or organising recreational activities. There are also a few images of places the battalion visited, like Folkestone aand Dover, where they bivouacked.[46]

Interspersed among the sketches are occasional pages of hand-written text, describing particular impressions or incidents. The text is descriptive and also conveys a real sense of the sights, sounds and emotions being experienced, which serves to enrich the words of the official 7th Battalion history. One of these passages describes the 'recruiting fever' he witnessed when he enlisted at Chichester depot at the end of August:

> 'into its gates, overflowing the wooden huts and spilling the men from every conceivable shelter, out on to the parade ground and wherever else they might find a place to sleep, came the men who formed the first Battalion of the Royal Sussex Regiment of the New Army.'[47]

In contrast the Battalion history talks briefly about 'the inrush of recruits everywhere and the temporary confusion resulting therefrom…'[48] Ralph goes on to say that stores soon ran out and some recruits spent their first few weeks in civilian clothes, a situation confirmed in the 7th Battalion history, which describes the shortages of clothing and equipment throughout the autumn of 1914. Thanks to the commanding officer, Colonel Osborne's, insistence, the battalion acquired supplies of many thousands of articles including shirts, cutlery, towels, razors, hairbrushes and socks from civilian sources.[49]

After a period of 'stiff training' at Colchester the battalion moved to Shorncliffe in Kent to join the other battalions that were to form the 36th Infantry Brigade of the 12th Division, by which time Ralph had been promoted to Lance Corporal. As the weather deteriorated in the autumn of 1914, with continual rain and sickness making things very difficult, they moved to Sandling near Maidstone to a hut encampment, but the conditions in the huts were even worse than being under canvas. In mid December, preparations were made for the brigade to be billeted in Folkestone, where they received a warm welcome, although the accommodation was variable. Training continued and according to the Battalion History much valuable experience was gained by digging trenches under all conditions – rain, cold and darkness – and by taking part in combined field exercises with other battalions in the Brigade.[50]

---

[46] WSRO Add. Mss. 25002: 12.
[47] WSRO Add. Mss. 25002: 7.
[48] Rutter [n.d.]: 4.
[49] Ibid: 5.
[50] Ibid: 9.

At the beginning of March they left Folkestone, where they were congratulated by the townspeople for their 'splendid behaviour' and for being quiet and considerate guests. To gain experience of moving and working as a division, which entailed organising their own billeting and supply columns, they marched to Aldershot. For Ralph the six-day march was 'perhaps the most thoroughly enjoyed and interesting' of all the days spent in training. As well as the excitement and anticipation of journeying on a strange road, Ralph describes the stirring feeling of being part of a mass of marching men, all moving forward in the 'rhythm of the regulated step', encouraged by drums and singing. Even as weariness set in and their packs and equipment grew heavier, they pulled themselves together when passing through towns and villages lined with cheering crowds.[51] As well as teaching these volunteer soldiers to fight, the training period served to create a fighting force of men with a sense of pride and loyalty to their unit and their comrades.

Training continued during the spring of 1915 and Ralph continued to make sketches of the people and places he visited. The time was approaching when the battalion would be ready to travel to France. Within nine months a group of raw civilians had been transformed into a fighting battalion. At the end of May they finally departed for France on SS Victoria from Folkestone, arriving in Boulogne on June 1st.[52]

By the time the 7th Battalion arrived in France in June 1915 the war had been underway for ten months. After the mobile phase of fighting, which lasted from August to December 1914, both sides dug in and a system of trenches stretched all the way from the Belgian coast to the Swiss border. In the majority of cases the Germans had fallen back to the most advantageous defensive positions, where they had built strong fortifications and deep trenches. Because the Allied forces saw the situation as temporary, their defences were less permanent and were often situated in less advantageous locations. The Belgian army defended the northern section of the Western Front. The British army, along with troops from all over the Empire, held the line from Ypres in Belgium to the River Somme in Picardy and the French army had the longest section from the Somme to the border with Switzerland.

For many of the men, including Ralph, this was the first time they had been abroad and his accounts of the first few days in France are infused with a sense that they were embarking on an adventure. He recalls waking up on his first sunny morning in France, with the 'glittering sea and the country that reminded one a little of our own Sussex Downs'. As they marched out of the town in the afternoon he describes them as a 'cheerful singing crowd out on a pleasure trip pleased with the novelty of new sights but never quite forgetting the real purpose of our coming'.[53]

---

[51] WSRO Add. Mss. 25002: 13.
[52] Sources of information about Ralph's military career: WSRO Add. Mss. 25001; Rutter [n.d.]: 1-12; TNA WO 339/83413.
[53] WSRO Add. Mss. 25002: 16.

As well as the interesting new scenery they passed on their journey to Blendeques, the men also experienced the hardships of travelling on an overcrowded troop train, and experienced the 'strange ways' of the French Railway, which Ralph describes humorously on page 17. Volume I ends as the Battalion leaves Blendeques, where they could hear faintly the sound of the guns. A two-day march, the second of which saw many men collapse with 'heat and fatigue', brought them to a rest stop from where they experienced their 'first sound of heavy gunfire and at night how near the rattle of machine gun and rifle fire appeared to be'.[54] The Battalion was marching to war.

[54] Ibid: 18.

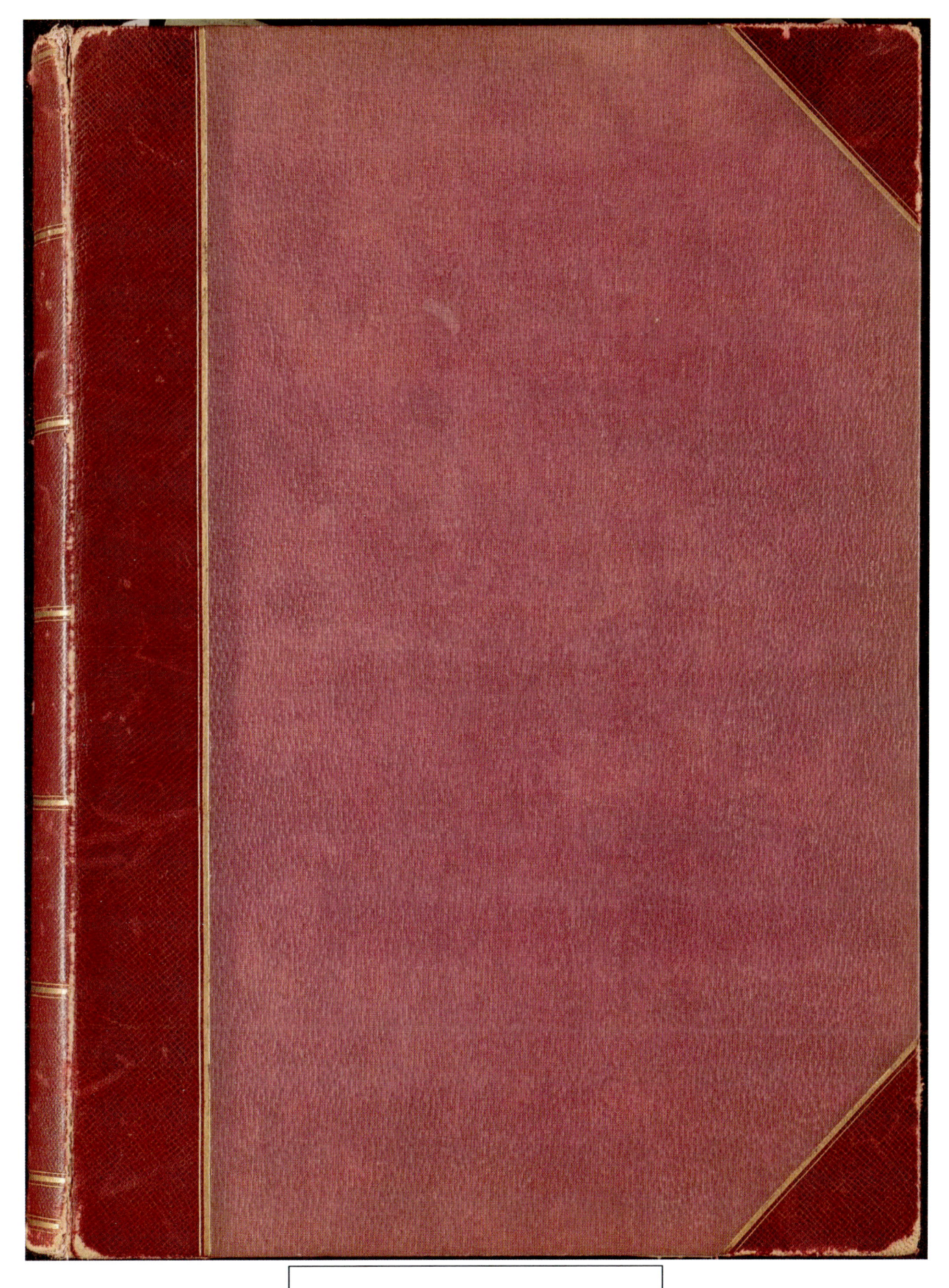

Front cover: Memoir Vol. 1

Colchester. August – September 1914.

It was here that the 7th Battalion Royal Sussex Regiment was formed. Commanded by Lieut. Col. W. L. Osborne.

The Depot at Chichester was the receiving station and into its gates, overflowing the wooden huts and spilling the men from every conceivable shelter out on to the Parade Ground and wherever else they might find a place to sleep came the men who formed the first Battalion of the Royal Sussex Regiment of the New Army.

Drafts left day after day for Colchester, as quickly as they could be "sworn in" and fitted, the "swearing in" was complete enough but the fitting of clothes was not nearly so and stores quickly gave out altogether so that many spent their first few weeks with the Army in their civilian outfit, or, which was worse, part civilian and part 'khaki.'

The journey to Colchester was marked by the great welcome London gave to us, cheering our way from one Station to the other, but the Barracks quickly enveloped us and stiff training was the daily programme, N.C.O's from the old 2nd Battalion [then fighting in France] assisting in this work and I think that their duties were made lighter by the willingness and keenness shewn by every man in spite of the number of "Parades" each day, the newness and roughness of the living and the unaccustomed discipline of the training.

It was a proud day to all when the whole Battalion first formed up and wheeled out of the Barrack square in "Column of Route," this too marked the close of the first chapter of our training, we had passed out of the nursery stage.

A corner of the Barrack Room, Colchester.

Firing recruits course at Hythe Ranges.

St Martins Plain & Sandling Oct. Nov. & Dec. 1914.

From Colchester the Battalion entrained to Shorncliffe going under canvas on St Martins Plain with the 8th & 9th Royal Fusiliers and the 11th Middlesex Regts which formed together with our Battalion of the Royal Sussex the 36th Infantry Brigade.

Fine weather, more interesting Parades and sea bathing made those first weeks very enjoyable, but the rains came and flooded the Plain so that it more nearly resembled a morass, yet even here it is easier to forget the crowded tents, our despairing efforts to keep clean and the Orderly Corporals greater desperation at issuing rations and food amidst that sea of mud, than it is to forget the good fellowship which existed in every tent.

Towards the end of November however we were marched to the new Hut Encampment at Sandling and expected to enjoy a drier and less muddied existence, but it was soon proved to us that tents could give points to "contract huts" in keeping out the rain, quite a few owing to the joyous way in which the water poured through, in its seeming efforts to drown us, often while we slept, had to be abandoned or given over to the Builder again.
"Duck-boards" were first introduced to us here, keeping us as in the Trenches [sometimes] clear of the mud.
It was while at Sandling that a good deal of real or imaginary? "Wind-up" occured about a hostile landing and much time was spent in Route Marching through Romney Marshes, each man carrying 100 rounds of Ball Ammunition and in digging Trenches by the canal, which curiously, had been dug years before in anticipation of a similar design on the part of the French.
In the second week of December, owing to the state of the huts and condition of the ground preparations were made for billeting the Brigade in Folkestone.

My platoon Sergt. and a favourite expression.

Folkestone · Jan · Feb · Mch · 1915 ·

Although billets may be looked upon from an official point of view as the last method of quartering troops to be adopted for any length of time, we considered it excellent, of course the billets varied, from the good middle class home to the large dilapidated Boarding House taken for the occasion by an enterprising couple and billeting anything from 30 to 60 men, it is unneccessary to add that the 2 or 3 in the former house enjoyed much the best time and in many cases making lasting friendships with those on whom they were billeted.

Fresh quarters invariably marked another stage in our Military life and appeared so noticeable not only in our own but in other units round about us, this vast number of recruits so swiftly developing into a thoroughly equipped and well disciplined Army, and here the growth seemed to have quickened for whereas before we had performed our various drills chiefly as a squad, Platoon or Company, now almost every day headed by the drums we marched out to the hills between Folkestone and Dover and about "Cæsar's Camp" and at the close of the operations, may be, the whole Brigade could be seen uncoiling itself and winding down the white road back into Folkestone. Five months old troops, having then the appearance in equipment and bearing of fully trained men.

SUSSEX SOLDIERS AT FOLKESTONE.

The troops, including the 7th Batt. Royal Sussex Regiment, who have been billeted at Folkestone for the past few weeks are now leaving the town, and interesting correspondence is published which has passed between the Mayor of Folkestone, Sir S. Penfold, and General Spens, commanding the 12th Division. The Mayor expresses on behalf of the people of Folkestone the appreciation felt locally of the splendid behaviour of the men. "I hear on all hands, from those who have had men billeted upon them, of the quiet, considerate conduct of the men, and how they have tried to cause as little inconvenience as possible, and the Chief Constable also speaks in high terms of the men's behaviour. Our hearts go out in feelings of deepest gratitude to all—officers, non-commissioned officers, and men—for what they are doing and are prepared to do and suffer for King and country; and that God may bless, protect, prosper them and bring them back safely is the earnest prayer of myself and the people of Folkestone."

General Spens replies in like complimentary terms, saying that "such a spirit of cordiality, co-operation, and such good feeling at such a time as this between civilians and soldiers is surely a proof that we all have in view a determination to work out a successful issue to the present condition of affairs."

Folkestone Pier and Harbour.

Dover Cliffs and the Coast Line from Folkestone to Dover.

Folkestone · Aldershot · March 1915.

Of all the days spent on training perhaps the most thoroughly enjoyed and interesting were the six days march from Folkestone to Aldershot.

Marching out one cold morning past the friendly crowds of Folkestone people out on to the road to Ashford our first halt.

To those who love a tramp on a strange road that bends and twists or stretches away before one, ever enticing one on and exciting the imagination with what is before, no ordered crush of marching men may take that delight away and in some ways but adds to it, for there is a feeling of being a part of one great forward moving thing, the regulated step, the ranks of men in front and those behind, one must move forward with it, the drums too and the singing men help to carry one through the lesser, feet weary, pack aching moments. How we pulled ourselves together when passing through the Towns and little villages where the school children cheered and the young men drifted out of sight.

From Ashford the route led us on through Kent to Maidstone and Edenbridge, from which place began our longest days march to Dorking, it was on the road nearer the latter Town that Kitchener watched us pass by, we were _his_ men and needed no Officer ordering us to "smarten ourselves" on marching past, men with a limp straightened up as though on Ceremonial Parade and in this way we entered Dorking too, we were rather proud of ourselves at the end of that 25 mile day.

One more halt at Guildford, another march across the "Hogs Back" and we were pouring ourselves into that cauldron of militarism, Aldershot.

Aldershot. March. April. May. 1915.

We had reached the final stages of our training and one remembers many long days of marching and manœuvring, of one Division out against another, over the large open gorse grown places, through wooded parks, wayside farms and little villages, of nights too in trenches, bivouacing on open commons and one great night when we built a huge wood fire and wrapping ourselves in our blankets, forming a huge circle about it, slept, waking early the following morning with the white frost covering us, refreshing ourselves in the clear cold stream near by and moving off as the sun rose for further practise in all the art of warfare.

Hard days, Great days, fit training for greater, harder days to follow.

Cooks getting busy during Field Operations.

31st May. Departure from England.

A day of great heat, many fatigues, cleaning of barracks and then wait-wait-wait in the sweltering sun for the order to move off. One would imagine that the marching away to war would be accompanied with band playing and excited, cheering crowds; the very opposite happened, but few civilians saw us as we marched away a Platoon at a time, loaded more than ever before with kit and blanket; glad enough to pitch the whole lot in the train and be done with it for a while and watch the green, lovely country of England being swept away from us untill we reached Folkestone and darkness with orders for no shouting or singing, but our old friends knew of our coming, gave us a cheer as we passed through to the harbour, thence on to the boat in a slow moving well shepherded flock that swore little and was soon packed away into every available space.

Many slept, a few wondered if they would pass that way again, and, go to France.

June 1st 1915. France.

We landed in darkness stumbling and groping our way over the lines and between the trucks and stores that cast deep black shadows in our way, out of the harbour where with a little cursing from the N.C.O.'s. we were formed up and marched up, up, out of the Town, and that hill has never seemed steeper with its border of houses deep in shadow, lifeless, except for a window here and there lighted and opened and head thrust out to see these heavy tramping feet pass by.

I remember next the awakening in the morning by someone shouting café and the sun trying to pierce through the canvas of the tent, then the view of glittering sea and country that reminded one a little of our own Sussex Downs.

We were to see a little more of Boulogne before moving up and that afternoon marched through its streets a cheerful singing crowd out on a pleasure trip pleased with the novelty of new sights but never quite forgetting the real purpose of our coming.

Of course we were greatly interested in the scenery that we passed on this our first Railway journey in France, but this sketch fails to convey the "comfort" experienced too [not that one expects comfort on Active Service]. The trucks are packed full with men and their kit, hopelessly full, no one can sit down or move it seems, the engine ahead gives one awful shriek, the trucks before move suddenly, the one you are in moves more suddenly and down you all sit, somewhere!. This sort of thing happening frequently has the effect of shuffling the whole conglomeration of men and kit into a better state of packing.
The train stops about every 10 minutes and for any length of time from 5 minutes to a couple of days, if you think it is going to stop long enough for you to get out and stretch your cramped limbs and do so, it immediately makes off at great speed for another 500 yards, but this being our first journey we were unfamiliar with the strange ways of the French Railway so we arrived at Blendecques very very cramped sore and dirty.

Nº 9 Platoons Billet.

A day or twos rest at Blendecques, where we faintly heard the sound of the guns and then to the road again, the first days march was uneventful but the following is worthy of mention being the worst we had experienced, it was a day of intense heat, the cheif cause of trouble, we were carrying all our kit and the distance, a little more than it should have been, proud as we had been of our marching abilities not more than half hung on to the finish, halts had to become longer and more frequent, but the men literally "fell out" of the ranks unconscious with the heat and fatigue, for the last mile before reaching the above little billet the roadside was littered with exhausted men. But I best remember the few days spent resting here the little orchard where a few of us slept and lived prefering to the stuffy over inhabited barn, the first sound of heavy gunfire and at night how near the rattle of machine gun and rifle fire appeared to be.

The cooking stove at a Farm near by, a favourite rendesvous for supper.

Corner of our Billet near Steenwerckes but it does not convey (fortunately) the smell from the midden.

Steenwercke, better seen at a distance.

VOLUME II

The second volume of Ralph Ellis's memoir covers the period from June to September 1915, when the 7th Royal Sussex was in northern France close to the Belgian border. According to his Officer Service Record, early in June Ralph was promoted to Lance Sergeant, although he was not paid for this new role until October.[55] During this period the men underwent further training and had their first experiences of trench warfare. As well as physical training, with many long route marches, the battalion received instruction in necessities such as the use of anti-gas respirators.[56] The Germans had first used poison gas on 22nd April 1915, at the start of the Second Battle of Ypres, and the protection was at first basic – a strip of gauze and a pad soaked in a solution to absorb the gas – but shortly afterwards an early type of smoke-helmet was issued.[57] The 7th Battalion War Diary also mentions training in 'rapid loading and aiming' of rifles (the standard British Army issue was the bolt-action, magazine-fed Lee-Enfield) and in 'bomb throwing with dummies', as well as equipment checks.[58]

In mid June (recalled by Ralph as later in the month) the battalion was attached to experienced units of the 82nd Brigade, each company serving in rotation for a 24-hour period. Ralph records this experience with the 1st Royal Irish Regiment and especially the first casualty suffered by the battalion: one of his comrades in 'C' Company was killed on 13th June.

On 27th June, a memorable day in the 7th Battalion's history, they went into the front line for the first time as a complete unit.[59] The trenches they took over were in a quiet part of the line at Le Touquet, near Armentières. During the four years of stalemate different sectors varied hugely, depending on what was going on at the time: the Somme was a quiet sector prior to 1st July 1916, when it became one of the deadliest of the entire war, similar to Arras until 9th April 1917, when a major offensive started. As described by Ralph, at this point in the war civilians were still living and working, as best they could, in towns and villages close to the front line. For the troops this provided some comfort as shops and estaminets or bars were close at hand. However, due to fears of espionage, during the summer of 1915 many of these areas were cleared.[60] On 9th September the 7th Battalion War diary records civilians being evacuated from the town of Houplines, nearby Le Touquet having been cleared at the end of June.[61] The evacuation was also for the safety of the local population: in the passage entitled 'The

---

[55] TNA WO 339/83413.
[56] WSRO RSR MSS/7/11.
[57] Rutter [n.d.]: 14.
[58] WSRO RSR MSS/7/11: 21 June 1916.
[59] WSRO RSR MSS/7/11; Rutter [n.d.]: 17.
[60] Rutter [n.d.]: 30.
[61] WSRO RSR MSS/7/11.

Bridge at Houplines' Ralph describes how children innocently playing in the river were in danger from machine gun fire, although he also mentions that the locals were always 'suspect to the British and in much danger from the Huns'.[62]

The battalion soon got used to life in the trenches around Armentières and Ralph describes the period here as smooth and uneventful. When not involved in an offensive, men in the front line of the British trench system – also called the firing line – followed a routine: half an hour before dawn was 'stand to' (short for stand to arms), when the men were on high alert for an enemy attack, followed by a rum ration and then a further 'stand to' half an hour after daylight, after which there was breakfast. In the morning they cleaned their equipment, which was often caked in mud, and cleaned themselves as best they could, as well as maintaining the trenches and other chores. If things were quiet they might get a hot meal at lunchtime and then have a period of rest in the afternoon, but a proportion of the men were always on duty, mainly as sentries. After tea was 'stand to' again, half an hour before dusk and then again half an hour after. Sleep was always in short supply.

It was at night that the real work took place. Ralph says the men were kept busy with 'arduous fatigues', 'improving defences' and there was 'plenty of excitement at night, working in No Man's Land'.[63] With the German trenches only 100 yards or so away, the defensive work carried out by both sides had to be done under cover of darkness. This was also an area with a good deal of mining and tunnelling, so saps and listening posts were constructed far into no man's land, almost to the enemy's front line. As well as the constant task of digging and repairing trenches, wiring parties went out into no man's land to check and repair the barbed wire defences and patrols went out to check out the enemy's defensive activities. Supplies of ammunition, equipment, food and water had to be carried up to the front line and every six days or so the battalions had to be relieved by fresh troops.

Battalions, working as a part of the larger army units of brigade and division, were regularly rotated in and out of the line. Typically (when not taking part in an offensive) they would spend up to six days in the front (firing) line directly facing enemy trenches, then move back to the support line and into reserve, during which time they undertook chores, fatigues and training, as well as being on standby in case of attack. After that they had a period of rest behind the lines, which gave them time to catch up on writing letters, playing sport, sampling local hospitality, and in Ralph's case, painting and drawing.

The 7th Royal Sussex quickly established this routine and according to the Battalion War Diary was in the firing line for an average of six days per tour, making a total of 48 days out of 91 days. For the remainder of the time they were in the support line and in

[62] WSRO Add. Mss. 25003: 39.
[63] WSRO Add. Mss. 25003: 27.

reserve, with no proper periods of rest. For the most part being in support and reserve removed the men from immediate danger of death and injury, but the most intensive bombardment Ralph records in this volume occurred while they were in the support line. It was a terrifying experience, vividly described. Most of the time the men were engaged in hard physical labour; the construction and repair of trenches, carrying parties bringing equipment and supplies up to the front line and many other jobs, so there was no chance of a rest.

Billets for a battalion of 800 to 1000 men were hard to come by so they had to sleep where they could, often outside in the summer months. The War Diary states that the 21st and 22nd August were the first two consecutive nights the men had spent inside in billets since 15th July and there were some wet periods, despite it being summer.[64] It is easy to see why, for Ralph, time spent in billets was treasured. While officers were often billeted in houses and slept in beds, the men were accommodated in large spaces like factories, breweries and even a coal mine, making themselves as comfortable as possible, often on the floor. There are several references in this volume, both sketches and text, to the cosiness and wellbeing Ralph felt when in a warm, dry billet with his comrades, particularly exemplified in the extract entitled 'By the light of the candle', which affectionately describes the scene and his feelings. As the battalion moved south at the end of September into the industrial heartland of France, they were billeted for a night in an uninviting coal mine, which, despite the dust and noise he describes as a 'warm snug billet', acknowledging that the alternative is sleeping outside where the 'cold wet wind sweeps through.'[65]

As well as the opportunity to rest, eat hot food and communicate with loved ones in Blighty, stays in billets offered a chance to bathe or wash and change clothes. Ralph describes arriving at a still-operational factory in Armentières straight from the trenches 'smelling strong of the earth' and plunging straight into big tubs, feeling 'the exhilaration and joy of becoming clean once more'. During the summer months the men also bathed in rivers close to the lines, which could be hazardous as one officer in the battalion was hit by a sniper as he emerged from the water, sustaining an injury in his backside.[66]

Life in the trenches was a constant battle not only against the Germans, but also with the other creatures with which the men had to cohabit. Rats were a constant nuisance, as were mice, which 'ate your food', but for many men it was the 'chats' or lice that were the worst annoyance, as they 'ate you'.[67] Conditions in the trenches with large groups of men living in close proximity in unhygienic conditions were ideal for lice to thrive. Simply washing bodies and clothes did not eliminate these creatures so during

[64] WSRO RSR MSS/7/11.
[65] WSRO Add. Mss. 25003: 43, 57.
[66] Rutter [n.d.]: 29.
[67] WSRO Add. Mss. 25003: 33.

quiet periods men would sit together running a flame down the seams of their clothes to kill the lice – a possible derivation of the term 'chatting'. As well as causing considerable discomfort, lice were the carriers of trench fever – a debilitating illness that reached epidemic proportions among the British and troops of other nationalities.

If periods away from the firing line gave the men some, albeit brief, feelings of security, it was devastating when the destruction of enemy fire shattered that illusion. On 27th September as the battalion moved south they passed through Armentières, spending the night in a large school and adjacent buildings. Having forgotten the war for a few blissful hours, with no warning the billets came under attack from shell-fire. For Ralph it was the intensity of the completely unexpected bombardment that was so shocking. According to the Battalion History, all the billets were hit, but the old school suffered worst. In total four were killed with eighteen wounded, and it was suspected that the Germans had been tipped off about the battalion's presence.[68]

After three and a half months in a 'quiet sector', the battalion had gained valuable frontline experience and had seen plenty of action. However, even in this 'comparatively pleasant' sector there were casualties; aside from sickness, forty were killed and seventy-three injured, making a total of 113 casualties.[69] With constant danger from sniper fire, it was particularly hazardous for the inexperienced who failed to keep their heads down. Tin helmets did not become standard issue in the British army until 1916. The action was intermittent with both sides initiating and retaliating. There were even some attempts by the Germans at fraternisation, which was forbidden by the British authorities. As well as snipers, machine guns, bombs and mines there were occasional periods of intensive shelling. Both sides were constantly developing new weapons, some with greater success than others. The Germans introduced a 'new form of abomination in the shape of incendiary shells'.[70] The British, meanwhile, had developed catapults for propelling missiles into the enemy's trenches, with varying degrees of success. Even the official 7th Royal Sussex Battalion History describes the demonstrations of these weapons as 'unintentionally hilarious' and quotes Ralph's account of the proceedings.[71] When firing the catapult, the primed missile (bomb or grenade) had a habit of falling back into the British trenches, causing the men to 'make a quick getaway', while tins of bully beef, used for practice, flew perfectly over the 90 yards into the German trenches. Although some found this amusing, Ralph did not as it was happening outside his shelter.[72]

The battalion's last tour in the front line at Houplines coincided with the start of the British offensive further south at Loos and their role was to stage a diversionary attack.

---

[68] WSRO RSR MSS/7/11; Rutter [n.d.]: 32.
[69] Rutter [n.d.]: 32.
[70] Ibid: 28: .
[71] Ibid: 30.
[72] WSRO Add. Mss. 25003: 72.

On morning of 25th September 1915 damp straw was lit on the parapet and smoke bombs were fired, but it seems the Germans were not deceived. The next day the battalion was relieved and started its journey to the south.[73]

Volume II of Ralph's memoir is composed of sketches interspersed with slightly longer captions and an increasing number of pages of handwritten text, some of which have been added later. Although this volume adheres to the basic chronology of the battalion's movements, it is composed of a series of observations, impressions and incidents that serve as captions for his sketches, or provide more detailed information. Incidents seem unrelated and there are passages describing the countryside, billets or dugouts, juxtaposed with accounts of shelling and death in the trenches, which illustrate the multitude of impressions that overwhelmed Ralph when first confronted with war. His comrades were his favourite subjects, drawn during quieter moments either resting or engaged at various activities, both while in the trenches and, more often, behind the lines, but never while engaged in action. One of the few 'action' sketches is of stretcher-bearers lifting a wounded man into a trench, a scene he graphically describes on the previous page in the passage 'Hit! Out in front'.

Many of the sketches are of the landscapes and buildings Ralph observed during the summer of 1915. Although the effects of the war are not immediately obvious in his landscapes, because they were often sketched away from the front line, many of the house and farms he drew had suffered considerable damage from artillery shell-fire.

In this volume it starts to become obvious that, while always an artist with an artist's eye for detail, words were becoming Ralph's favoured medium. His drawings could not convey all that he was seeing and experiencing, but words could. As well as describing his experiences as a soldier, he uses words to convey his impressions of the landscape and his surroundings.

When he recalls deserted homes where the inhabitants have fled at a moment's notice, he notes small details like an uneaten meal or three pairs of clogs belonging to the absent family, bringing a human dimension to the scene. In a description of a 'Thatched farmhouse in the meadows by the River', which accompanies an image, he takes comfort from the power of nature to survive in a landscape damaged by war. Here, as in many of his descriptions of nature, the language becomes lyrical and romantic with roses blooming in a tangle of 'wild and beautiful lovliness' [sic] and 'a pheasant as bright as the morning' which 'slithered through the purple mass of thistles.'[74]

It is likely that during this period Ralph started to work as an observer with the artillery. Although he makes no direct mention, in this volume he makes several references to visiting 'O Pips' or Observation Posts in chimneys or church spires, which

---

[73] Rutter [n.d.]: 31; WSRO Add. Mss. 25003: 52.
[74] WSRO Add. Mss. 25003: 49.

made ideal vantage points. Observers studied the enemy lines for evidence of machine gun and artillery positions and the information was then communicated to the British gunners who aimed to destroy the enemy positions. Later in his career Ralph became an Observation Officer. With his natural talent and precision and his ability to make quick sketches of what he saw, he was the ideal 'spotter' and this talent was to have a significant impact on his wartime experience.

Towards the end of June 1915 we left Steenwercke, marched to Pont de Nieppe and were attached, a Company at a time, to a Regular Battalion of the Royal Irish Regiment, who were then holding the line by Le Touquet, with the Bosch from 3 to 700 yards away, very quiet and unoffensive by day but more restive by night with Machine Gun and Rifle fire and an occasional spit fire of a "Whizz-Bang", this sort of thing we quickly found facilitates the digging of trenches during the fair intervals, at least down to a depth sufficient to cover one, but whilst the machine gun bullets are zip-zipping like mad, flying bees a few feet above the ground, how one flattens to the earth and feels like a mountain of flesh in a direct line of those stinging bees, but digging, grass cutting and wiring is dull business without a little excitement, it was thus we came by our first casualty buried there in the British Cemetry at Houplines to be joined later on by others of the Batt.

Shortly after our stay with the Royal Irish the 12th Division took over the Sector of Line from Ploegstreert Wood to just south of Houplines, our own particular bit of line being opposite Frelinghien not more than 100 yards from the Bosch. Life here ran almost smoothly and uneventful with much hard work at improving the defences but plenty of excitement at night working in No-man's-land, swept by much rifle fire, the constant flare of Very Lights, that at first seem to point at you with the personal touch of the Limelight... A good deal of sapping and mining was carried out here necessitating arduous fatigues and listening posts tunnelled out almost to the enemy front line, occasionally a mine was sprung, a sudden roar, the earth takes life and rocks for a moment, machine guns yap like angry terriers and all is quiet again.
These were the largest excitements of life in this Sector.

Houplines and River Lys.

A few shells were occasionally put into the town and it was not unusual at such times to see excited, gesticulating civilians at their doors peering to see where the last shell had burst while the more prudent made for cover and in the case of shop and estaminet keepers, snatching the contents of the till in their excited bolt to the cellar.

· · Remains of houses bordering the road from · · ·
Houplines to Frelinghien.

This part of the road was not more than 800 yards and in full view from the German front line, therefore it was with some surprise that we in our front line one afternoon beheld an Officer and orderly driving up this road in a mess-cart, they came within 600 yards of the Enemy Line, but the Hun message reached the Officer more quickly than our warning of danger could. The orderly got away with the cart, clattering back along the cobbled road at a great pace, the singing bullets urging on both man and mule.

This incident happened owing to the similarity of names of some French villages. The officer having orders to proceed to Frelinghien on a Bombing course and in spite of the protests of the sentry on the road at the outskirts of Houplines, would proceed.
The sentry was court-martialed but exonerated.

The Winding Front Line

Where the bales of sandbags are filled and piled high to build the breastworks, rot back to earth again and must be constantly renewed, they are the "driftwood" that make the high water line of War.

Hit! Out in front.

70 yards or so from the uneven line of enemy parapit. a stray bullet tears its way through the chest of a man, saping his strength in a moment, a stretcher is brought.

Inwardly you curse the War, the rain, the sticky clinging mud, the wire, the broken ground, the tins, refuse of the trenches and every other devilish thing that makes your progress a stumbling horror and to that moaning figure in the stretcher ?.

The bank of mud and slimy sandbags called a parapit is at last reached and we are into our own trench, free from the personalities of casual bullets but not from the slippery mud that takes control of your feet.

Oh God! how he groans and talks of the "Old Lady" his wife at home, he thinks of noone else, not of himself and the agony our stumbling feet have given him, he is certain he is going "West" three days later he has gone.

Died of ✝ Wounds.

The little border house by the bridge connecting France to Belgium.

This house so like a million other homes where a screaming shell has brought the horror of hell itself to those who lived there; no imagination is needed to see what happened as one peers through the splintered door, the needlework thrown aside, money box smashed everything else of their little world left in great haste lest the next shell bring an even greater hell.

Dug - outs.

When obtainable are <u>incidentally</u> for tired men to get into on every possible occasion and sleep, but a <u>home</u> for every creeping thing the earth breeds, our specialities here were "chats" and mice, the "chats" ate you and the mice ate your rations and if you were of a worrying nature there was always the possibility of a Bosch mine lifting beneath your dugout, apart from these petty annoyances one did enjoy little social gatherings, inviting pals round to a feed when a fat parcel arrived. The mice at least had to be defeated.

Deserted homes near the line and the Observation Baloon.

"To Let."

Part of Frelinghien burning

Clouds of smoke drift back over the lines, the black totured steel limbs of what had been thriving factories grin through, a red tongue of flame licks the air and is gone again, no sign of life, we can only guess at the purpose of the burning and what is happening behind the rolling bank of smoke.

At night such fires make a bloody banner of war waving over the dark level stretches of earth where men and transport are moving up and down to the line, are silhouetted against the flaming banner and curse its familiarity.

Factory Chimnies at Armentieres

These stalwart symbols of peace and industry were very near to the machinery of destructiveness, our own guns lay in a field adjoining one factory where coarse textile fabrics were still being manufactured by old men and girls in a very quiet unassuming way, here too came the men straight from the Trenches and smelling strong of the earth to rush and plunge like boys into the big tubs and feel the exhilaration and joy of becoming clean once more.

None of the stacks breathed smoke but some had eyes that saw far back into the German lines.

A deserted barge on the River Lys

How busy had been this waterway could be gathered from the number of barges that were left partly or wholely sunk in the river by fleeing owners who could not away quickly enough from the oncoming plague with these their moveable homes.

To one such barge we owed much, from it was fixed a diving board and here came the swimmers to dive and plunge to the envy of those who could not swim.

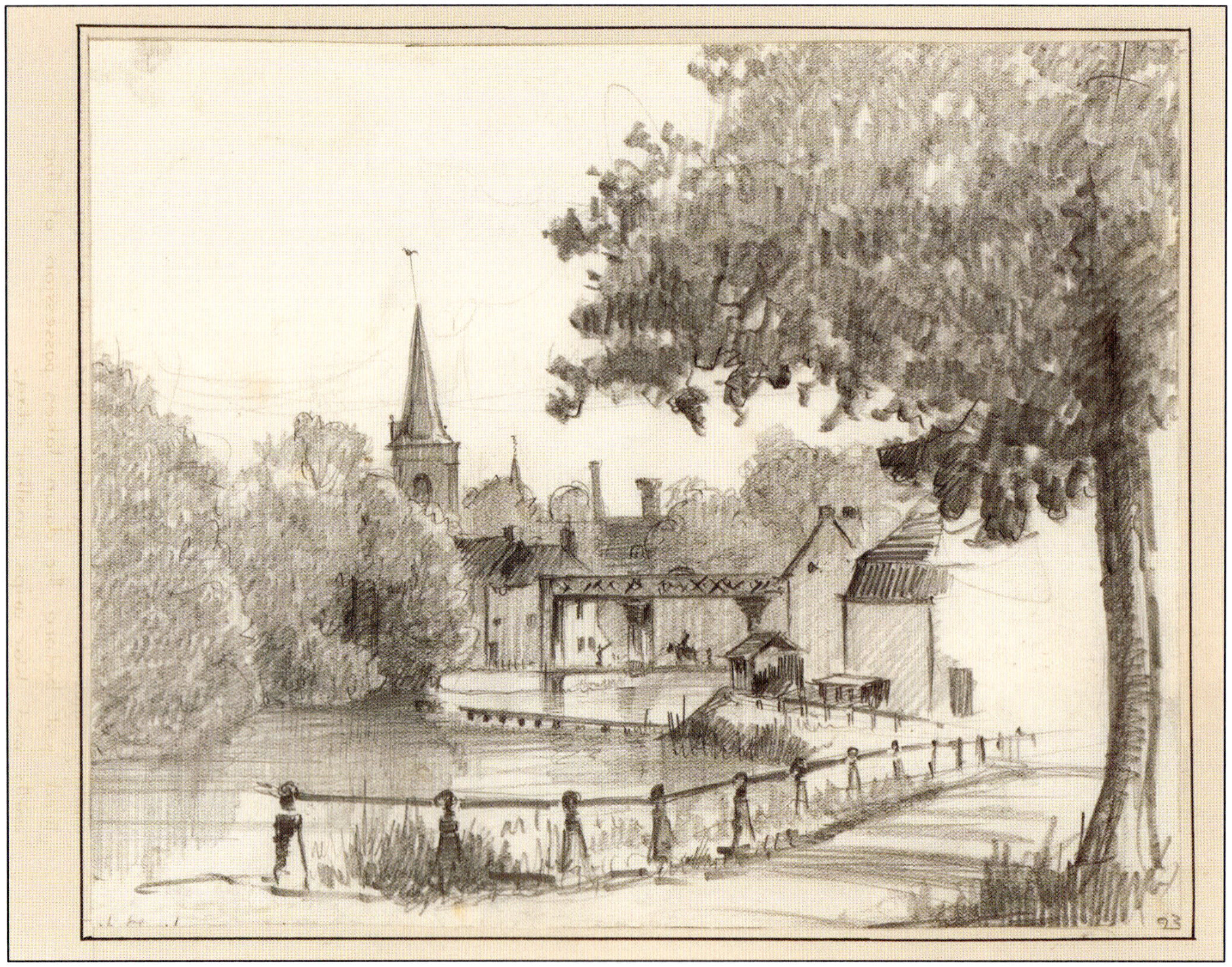

The Bridge at Houplines.

That carried the road into Belgium and up to the line. To the guard here came the duty of staying all civilians, for quite a few passed this way and on the Sunday morning, many came dressed sombrely in black with unsmiling joyless faces from one or two farms and little cottages even nearer the line than this, to worship here in Houplines, all had to shew their identification cards that none of us could rightly understand but they were always "suspect" to the British and much in peril from the Huns, how great a need of God?.

By the river side played the children unthinking of perils of war, such things come suddenly. Machine gun bullets slashed the water, cracked and spit with hate and venom on the stones, it is like a stampedeing horse striking the cobbles with its shod hoofs. a child screams, a womans high pitched terrified voice cries out and a door is banged with violence. The sentry stoops to pick up a small flattened piece of metal and drops it hastily with an oath.

It is but as a passing shower, the children must out to play again in the sunlight and the women to stand by the door for a moment or two and jabber excitedly.

When the day gives place to night, the sentries challenge "Halt! who are you?" rings out continually. The bayonet clinks with a ring as the butt of the rifle is brought to the ground and the challenged pass by. Fatigue parties coming down from the line to return with sandbags filled with the next days rations slung across their shoulders or laden with all manner of material for the building and defence of the entrenched line, other dark masses of men pass, going up to dig the pick and shovel faintly clinking against the slung rifle. These will return dirty and tired, just before the dawn takes possession of the earth and war grips another day.

Houplines from the Lock.

This sketch was taken in Midsummer 1915 whilst on guard duty by the lock. There was no "hate" that day except from the mouth of the old lock-keeper and his oft repeated story of the Huns visit back in '14. The sun poured out its colour and warmth over river and field, and to the little estaminet by the water side came the brewer and the baker as in days of peace but now putting their trust in the line of khaki men behind the sandbaged bank not more than a thousand yards away.

Milham.

"Rat" Morris.

L/c. Whittenstall.

Three of Nº 9 Platoon. the latter two have journeyed west.

A dug out and the Catapult.

The latter was an exciting method of throwing bombs for one could never be certain whether the bomb would strike against the bank and roll at your feet or be flung high into the air and drop bursting into the Bosch Trench as desired. We experimented with tins of "bully beef," occasionally making good shots and free gifts to the Hun. but when using a bomb, just releasing the spring then bolting for cover trusting this gift too might find a grey coated receiver.

By the light of the candle.

It is the close of a day back in 'support', some sleep already with waterproof sheet between them and the bricked floor of the building, greatcoat flung over and pack for a pillow, a few read, having something to read, many write to those at home, several groups are playing at cards. from them come an occasional tinkle of coins and many excited exclamations, while on their faces dwells a look which is oblivious to everything but the game, one lively crowd are joking and singing, a mixed bunch of men but birds of high spirit and light heart, thus they flock together.

Everywhere are the little flickering candles that pick out with high warm lights the features of the men and wrap them in dark mysterious shadows.

Section commanders call the roll of their sections all are reported present to the Orderly sergeant who reads out the orders for the morrow, one by one the lights go out the prone sleeping figures bunched together for warmth increase in numbers the card players are the last to give way to the pleasure of rest and sleep.

The lights have gone, one hears the cough of the sentry outside the dull thud of foot and clank of rifle and bayonet, it increases the feeling of snugness as one pulls the coat more closely around and finds a hollow spot for the hip bone, the night is ours to spend in luxurious sleep, the softest bed in the world cannot give you more than that.

———————

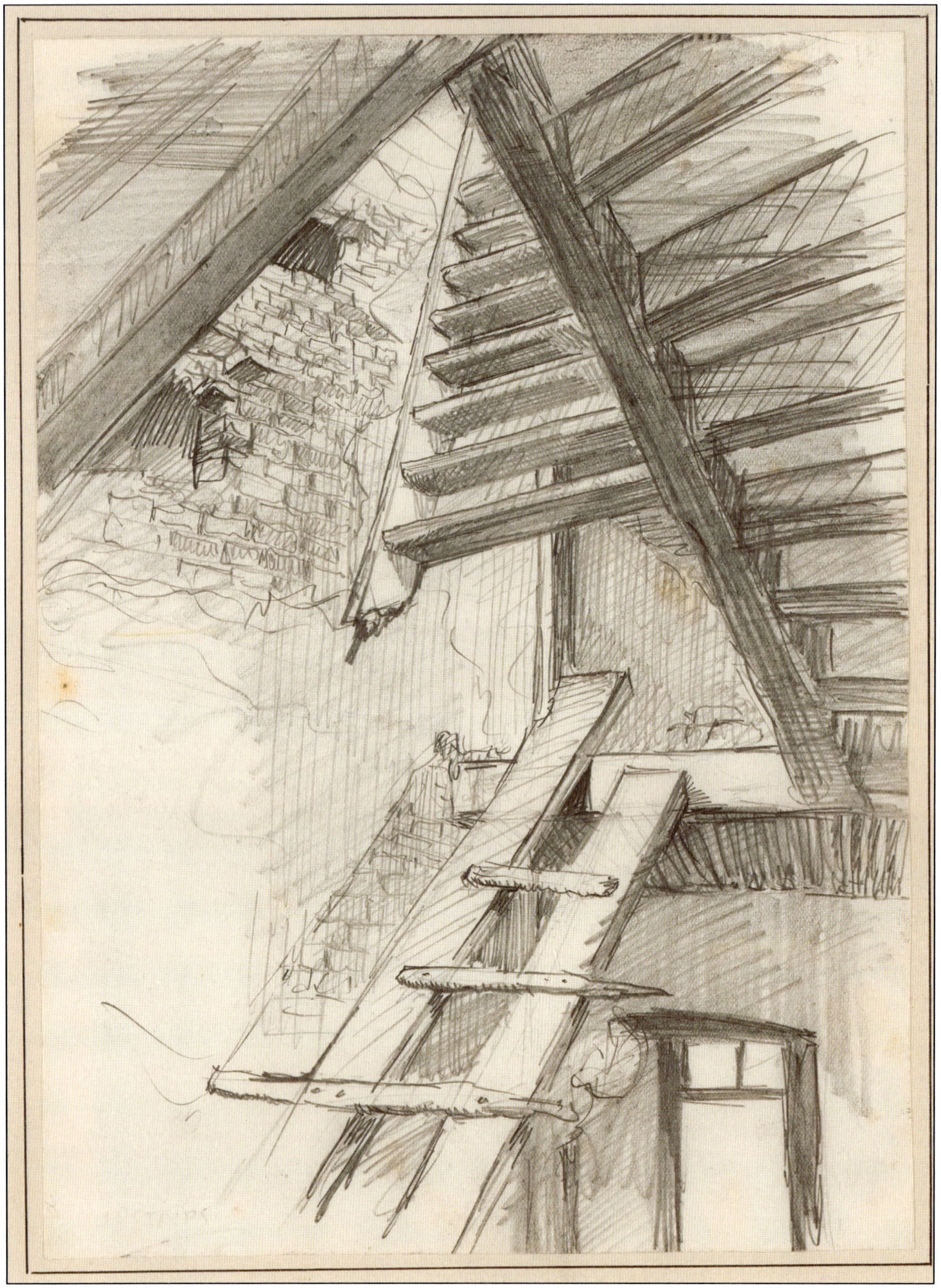

The way up to an Observation Post.

We reach the place by a narrow trench that would draw you back as you force your way through, it ends a little distance from the "Post". The remaining ground may be got over by any form of progress you like, keeping the "house" well between you and the eyes of the enemy. The ground floor is a shambles of broken bricks, rubbish and odds and ends of smashed household things, but gaping shell holes prevent any freedom of movement here and it is so as one clambers up the rough ladder and on to the broken staircase that begins at the first floor. It is a wonder how the walls hold together so often has it been pierced by screeching shells.

On the 2nd floor a hole has been made use of, it is sand-bagged about and covered carefully with canvas leaving room for the eye of the telescope to peer through, The observer is stretched out on boards placed across the ribs of the floor, sometimes he wonders how long such a "post" will be left by the Bosch and whether he will be on duty when the house breakers finish the job, but it is a good spot and there is much to interest one and to report upon. The country stretches away into the blue distance of wood and sloping hill untouched by War and one is tempted to devote ones sight to those more distant places of sunlight and shadow on green fields and red roofed cottages peeking through stately trees in mass and those that border the roadways and point them out to us so clearly, it is a beautiful lonely world back there.

Nearer are the ragged lines of our own and the enemy trenches, a hawk hovers high above the brown smudge of "No-mans-land" blending into red where the tangle of wire runs parallel to the line of trench. What sign of life in that front line? A bit of rubbish thrown over, a whiff of smoke occasionally and yet by these little signs do we get to know perhaps as much by instinct too when fresh troops occupy the line, other things and.

other observers corroborate, there is a bit of road back behind that leads up to their Communication trenches, it becomes visible between the gaps in the hedge and where the road runs higher. the Hun, careful man that he is tells us a few other things about himself, so we watch until one day a careless observer forgetful of the eye that is watching. watching too speaks to him of our little post in the house. the Hun observer tells the gunner who arranges a little shoot before lunch.

The clouds of dust and smoke rise pink and salmoned coloured high into the sunlit air, the house breakers have finished the job and we must find another O-Pip.

Edmeads Farm.

The support line ran about this old torn farm which still retained a little of its old dignity and an even greater importance than it held before. Its beauty had gone, the dyke surrounding it, its waters covered with a green and yellow slime of weed bore upon its surface the splintered and broken remains of beautiful trees, and there, a few bright coloured garden flowers set in a patch of fresh green grass give a hint of past glories and fairer garments.

The Hun worried the place occasionally making the observers drop from the beams and dive for cover in great haste.

Through the shell hole ... Frelinghien and the River Lys.

The Farm by the River.

The thatched Farm in the meadows by the River.

It stood away from the haunts of the workers in War, a little quiet peaceful place that attracted one always, peeping at it as one passed over the top of the zig-zagged scar of trench that hid us from view. It lay by the river side, the Hun ignored it, why waste shells? noone could approach or walk there without being seen. But one <u>had</u> to peep behind those walls to walk into that patch of garden where the roses bloomed, It was such a tangle of wild and beautiful louliness, we crept by the hedge. a pheasant as bright as the morning cried out in great alarm and slithered through the purple mass of thistles, we came upon old disused trenches hid from sight again by all the wild growing things that nature seems to heap together in great beauty to hide the scars that we have made. A rotting scotch glengarry and rusty mess-tin in a scooped out hollow by the hedge tell where the first of our men held up the Hun.

We wander through the rooms that are slovenly with dirt and the scattered things that noone needed. wooden clogs, these tell us a little of those who lived there. one pair big and roughly fashioned speak of a man knowing the earth, slow in thought and movement and with little imagination, another pair, smaller, less rudely finished with crude ornamentation cut into the face of them, a womans footgear perhaps it was she who tended the little garden of flowers and there was a much smaller pair almost shapely and decorated with a finer neatly cut pattern to please the wearer and the garden was made to please her too, for fair flowers and gardens are rare in the small Belgian farms.

The Farm by the River.

Rats scampered away through the straw as we walked through the cow stalls and bare barn peering here and there at the old implements belonging to the land. One shell had brought a mass of thatched roof tumbling into the little grass grown yard. A small round window high up like an eye to the barn tempted one to clamber up and peer through.

The meadows that stretched away to the German lines was the playground of the breeze it rippled and bent with an affectionate touch the tall loose growing grass and with the sunlight changing the shades of colour of its raiment a hundred times.

A no-mans-land, and beyond with scarce form or shape the broken buildings. bits of colour grey blue, red and yellow splashed in front with the green of trees and rising out of its chaos tall chimneys broken and pierced by shell fire and probably hiding eyes too that look and search for movement across that waste of land.

The Brasserie at Frelinghien

When we first came to live in the bit of trench not a 100 yards from the chalk and clay parapit that ran in front of the Brewery, it was suicide to lift ones head above the "bags". There were men who left us suddenly that way, one cleaning his rifle, humming a tune the while forgetful of the watchful sniper and the height of the protecting parapit, dropped to the bottom of the trench, the bullet lifting his field service cap and p the top of his skull with it, another in a similar way but fortunately only loosing his cap to his great consternation, annoyance and future guidance.

Our own snipers busied themselves from well chosen spots and the men too from the trench were keen with the rifle, worrying the Hun and checking the ardour of their crack shots, so that in our latter days here we could take greater liberties and it was the Hun that was most careful to keep his head well down, so one was able to make a quick sketch of that interesting mass of bricks and mortar without interference.

Came rumours of our leaving this quiet spot, of something big happening somewhere south of us. It _might_ extend, and for us would come the experience of moving forward into the beyond. We brought strange goods to the line un-warlike things, wes were not to fight the Hun but try to frighten him. [I think we amused him].

From away south came the rumbling of the guns thumping the air, the wind gently driving across to the Bosch lines, as we desired.

One forgets the time but not the array of big queer looking candles that had to be fired from the parapit and the trusses of damp straw to be lit and rolled over, it was going to be a big 5th of November day with lots of banging too of bombs that burst and threw little jets of blue flame about.

From a spectacular point of view it was a huge success, the straw was lit and pushed over as one, the grey and white smoke drifted away to the wondering Hun. Then the fun began merrily, running from point to point along ones section of trench lighting and placing the candles on the parapit, for a moment or two watching the smoke gush forth and form great volumes of gorgeous colour ranging from cream to deep salmon, hiding everything from view more than 30 yards away. Machine guns tap-tap-tapped and the bullets came cracking and swapping into the sandbags richocheing over the trench and away back. The Hun entered into the fun but his gunners treated us almost with contempt, a few rounds of shrapnel burst about us adding a little to the noise but more to the excitement of things. A bend of the trench gave a distant view of the line it looked as though the parapit were afire with the smoke cloud rolling away from it across no-mans-land.

The fun ceased as the fireworks gave out and things quickly became normal again, Fritz refused to be roused.

The following day orders were read out from Gen French that something had been successful, he thanked the troops, but we were soon to know more of that something.

The Brasserie at Frelinghien.

To the road again.

For the last 3 months we had lived very near to the Town of Armentieres but few of us had entered it since passing through on our way up.

We had better luck in the trenches, one expects to be shelled there it is an ever present possibility, in billets one shakes off the immediate presence of War so that if shells come they arrive with an intense, more dramatic shock.

Our first taste of really heavy shelling came not long before we left while in the support line. There had been fighting at Hooge and the Hun out of spite or "wind up" gave us an hours devoted attention.

We awoke, something had gripped the earth and shaken it with violence, there was no mistaking the cause, the shells came whinning up out of the distance developing in the last downward rush into a shriek of mad hate, a fraction of a moment of intense anxiety, then the cracking tearing burst biting into the earth and gripping it with the passion and violence of a mad devils beast, but the moments thrilling releif, that one was not for us. Clods of earth, the earth, mother of all flowering growing beauty is changed, thrown up out of itself and come to your feet with the same intense violent force of the jagged portions of metal that are hissing through the air too.

The day has but just begun, the shock of the sudden awakening and coldness of the early morning air makes one shake from head to foot, one strives with all ones power for control, it is a matter of minutes, it seems like hours before one is able to sit there and wait coolly, trusting in providence that no shell is booked for our shelter one cannot call it a dug-out there is but a foot of earth above the wood supports of the roof. to ones imagination it seems the resting place for a 5". again and again as the nearer shells approach one sees the momentary lightning flash, daggers of flame, the welter and chaos of earth and splintered wood. choking fumes of smoke. tearing bloody metal. mangled flesh. blood. and then ?.

There is a moments lull and up on the breeze is carried the music of a cocks crowing. one is looking out of hell through a small window and seeing far far away a vision of the fairest most peaceful things that one has ever known and but half realised.

The storm is all but over we hasten around to the other shelters where had rested the men of our sections and whatever had been there emotions they now sit smoking and laughing, happy in a new lease of life.

A large school was the last billet for the Battalion at Armentieres. we arrived full of glee at taking to the road once more and were to be allowed out for the one evening spent here properly cleaned and belted, a good pay out and a place to spend it in. A war did not exist, it was forgotten.

The men are just strolling back to billets, many are gathered in the large school rooms where they will sleep and others are in the open playground for they find greater amusement amongst themselves than elsewhere.

The least expected intense dramatic moment arrives stripped bare of any warning, a sudden hurricane of sounds at once, the bursting shell, and glass shattered into a million pieces, sounds like witches screaming laughter, and high above it all the penetrating terrified scream of a child, This grips and wrenches you out of your normal self more than all else.

Out to the entrance, a few men stand about in the school yard trying to look unconcerned.

In the arched way, one is instantly reminded of a butchers slaughter house, so much the blood flows over the cement floor. the men say and groan little. more field dressings are shouted for. the wounds are quickly bound up, one speaks of another that is outside on the pavement "Hit worse than me".

But the street is empty of every living thing, he was just a boy stalwart clean and good to look at, bitter hate of War takes hold of one as we carry him in.

We are "standing too" half the night but the morning brings the open road.

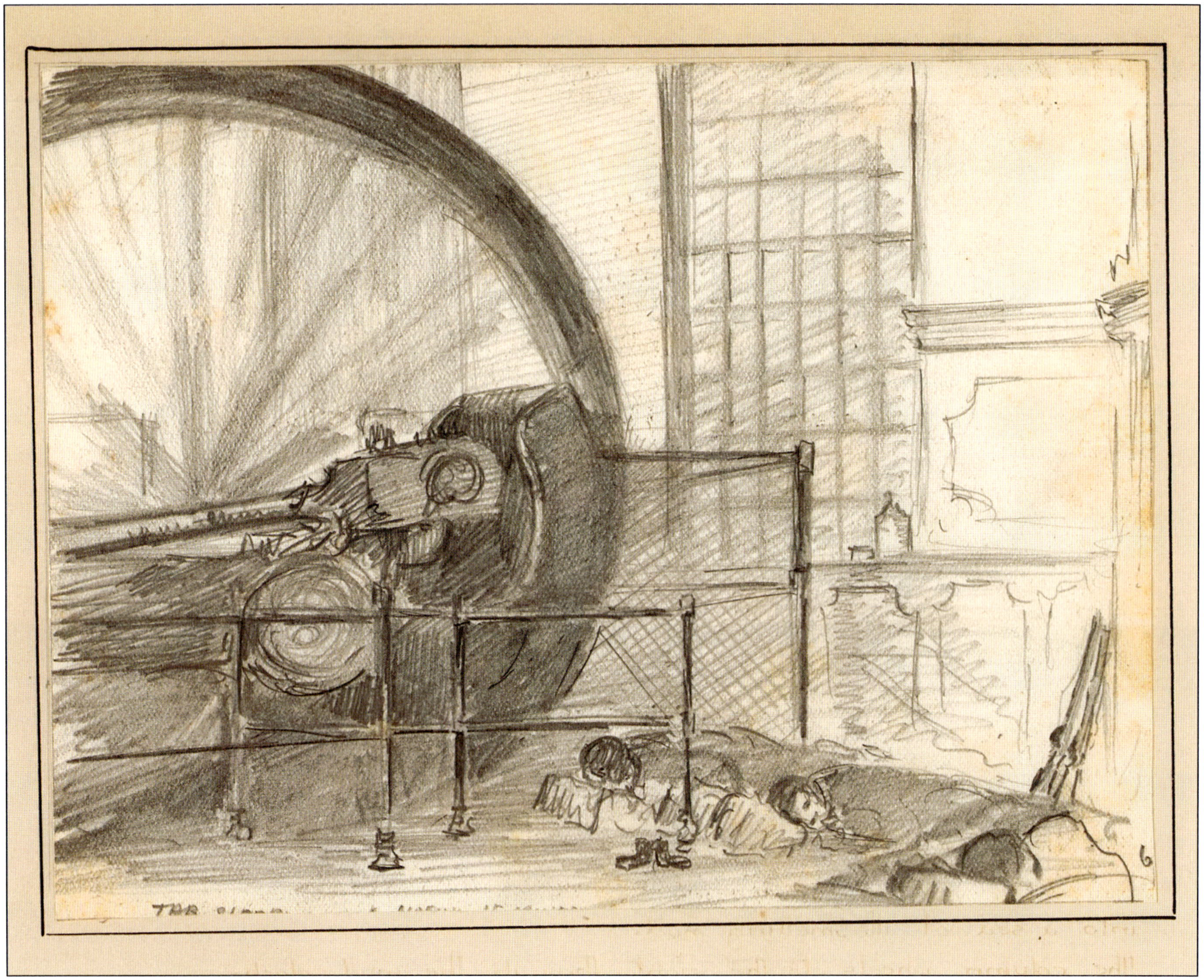

The billet at Noeux le Mines.

The road creeps back toward the line and the rain the accompaniment of every British "push" streams down, we round a corner of the road wooded on the left. a Divisional or Corps H.Q's. is here and some men of our 2nd Battalion are passed who give us short graphic bits of news, away to the right the ground drops then seems to run level as a plain. below is Noeux le Mines and the big ugly slag heaps and away in the distance we watch the white balls of smoke and know what awaits us there.

The last lap takes us through the dirty village where much transport has churned the surface of the road into a sea of ill smelling mud.

The column wheels to the right through the mud splashed gateway. so we are to be billeted in a coal mine, it does not look inviting, but anywhere for rest and sleep.

Our company is in luck we are in the large engine room a clean place smelling of oil, but warm so warm, others must sleep where the cold wet wind sweeps through or the dust of coal is always in the air and settles thickly on everything. Later we find time to watch the working of the mine and the black faced girls sorting the coal, a few of our men, miners from the north have energy to take up for an hour their old tasks, working arduously, wheeling and pitching the small trucks of coal that rise so swiftly up out of the bowels of the earth.

Back to our warm snug billet and the loud buzz and hum of the machinery which we thought might disturb us, nothing could keep us awake, the noise becomes a drone we are intoxicated with sleep for one more night.

VOLUME III

On 25th September 1915, the French and British armies launched a major offensive – The Big Push – intended to break through enemy lines and strike a decisive blow against the German Army on the Western Front. While French forces attacked in Champagne and Artois, the British advanced along a six-mile front between Loos and La Bassée. The industrialised coal mining area around Loos was difficult terrain for an offensive: the ground was flat and open, providing no protection from machine-gun fire and the many pit heads and slag heaps provided defensive positions, which were heavily fortified by the Germans. Many of the troops taking part were inexperienced volunteers and the supporting artillery was short of heavy guns and shells. For the first time the British deployed poison gas, although with mixed success due to the weather conditions. Despite heavy casualties, gains were made on the first day, but these were not exploited as the reserves were held too far away and the attack soon faltered.

By the time the 7th Royal Sussex entered the line on 30th September, there was a lull in the fighting. The Battalion had the 'honour' of relieving the 3rd Coldstream Guards, revered as elite troops, in trenches recently vacated by the Germans. According to the Battalion History it was a 'long and trying relief' with 'full packs, which made the march extremely tiring.'[75] As they moved up to the line they witnessed the reality of a major offensive: the utter confusion and congestion of supplies, equipment, horses, men, casualties and mud, all within range of the German artillery. These were Ralph's first 'real impressions of warfare… of its callous cruelty, waste and a little of its hardships'.[76]

The Battalion were to spend the next seven days consolidating the trench system in the new British line. At night large working parties constructed new defensive positions: the newly dug trenches, which were out in no man's land, were only three feet deep but had to be manned all day sitting or lying down. The men were not even allowed to smoke. To add to the discomfort, autumn arrived with rain, damp and cold. Ralph recollects how they buried the dead of both armies, observing the dramas played out before the moment of death, such as an officer and his men confronting two large Prussian soldiers, all of whom died together. He was also moved by the severed limbs they found among the debris, with no bodies attached. This period had a profound effect on Ralph: he recalls a wounded man in no man's land, waving a white rag, seven days after the attack. Rescue attempts had been made, but failed with fatal results. For him nothing illustrated more forcibly the 'brutality' of war, the sweeping away of civilisation and the return to a 'savage state'.

[75] Rutter [n.d.]: 34.
[76] WSRO Add. Mss. 25004: 66.

The 7th Royal Sussex left the line on the 7th October. Moving large quantities of men, equipment and supplies around was logistically complex, not least because it was always done under cover of darkness. Throughout the memoir Ralph's impressions of reliefs both in and out of the line are vivid; the confusion, the exhaustion, the dread, the anticipation of rest. They were dangerous operations, often in open ground away from the relative safety of the trenches. But he also captures the joy and 'lifting of spirits' of seeing the cooks and knowing that a hot cup of tea and breakfast were close by.

For the next six days the 7th Royal Sussex was in reserve, spending time in billets cleaning up. During this time a further attack was launched on Hulluch and the German stronghold, the Hohenzollern Redoubt, but although they were on standby, they were not required.[77] After another unpleasant relief on 14th October they were back in the firing line, opposite Hulluch, again employed improving trenches and burying the dead after the most recent attack, which according to the Battalion history was only partially successful.[78]

On the 19th October they were relieved and moved back into the old British front line at Hulluch. Ralph writes a fascinating account of an incident that occurred the next day in 'A fatigue to remember'. His company was detailed to carry large barbed wire entanglements up to the front line, to reinforce the defences in no man's land. Not only was it a near impossibility to carry these 'cumbersome abortions' in daylight over smooth ground, they were doing it in the dark, over shelled ground, littered with debris and dead bodies, or when that became too dangerous, in narrow overcrowded trenches. As they neared the firing line they came under shell-fire and had to abandon their cargo, instead joining a line supplying bombs to those ahead holding the firing line. Ralph later learned of the heavy casualties sustained and the fate of some of the men.[79] This incident is briefly mentioned in the Battalion War Diary and then in the official History of the 7th Battalion, but neither provides any clue about what it was like to be there, illustrating the value of Ralph's vivid memoir.

The 7th Royal Sussex was relieved on 21st October and moved to billets to clean up and for training (in throwing live bombs), but this was not to be a long rest as on 28th they were back in reserve trenches between Vermelles and Noyelles. With the onset of winter the weather deteriorated and it rained heavily and persistently, giving the Battalion their first real experience of French mud. The rain exacerbated the problem of low-lying boggy ground, with a very high water table, made worse by the destruction of the pre-war drainage infrastructure. The newly-dug trenches they occupied were in

[77] WSRO RSR MSS/7/11.
[78] Rutter [n.d]: 38-39.
[79] WSRO Add. Mss. 25004: 72-74.

a terrible condition: according to the Battalion War Diary, the men were in dugouts without trench boards (duck boards) and the accommodation was 'damnable'.[80]

Three companies, including Ralph's 'C' Company, were selected to mount an assault near the Hohenzollern Redoubt and spent several days practising on trenches specially constructed to represent those they would be attacking. On 5th November they took over front line trenches (aptly named 'Sticky' and 'Mud' Trench) and spent a couple of days doing heavy fatigues in pouring rain with no shelter. The appalling conditions began to take their toll and many men went sick with trench foot and rheumatism, greatly reducing the numbers fit for duty. Because of the weather, the planned assault was called off.

Ralph's account of this period does not appear chronologically in his memoir, but in the section entitled 'The Vermelles Sector', which is on page 90 of Volume III. His memories seem to have been prompted by the Battalion revisiting the sector in February 1916. In it he graphically describes what the men had to withstand, living in the open on the fire step for days on end, with only a waterproof sheet for shelter and often up to their knees in water. He praises the fortitude of the men who cheerfully bore the terrible hardships.

At this time trench foot became a serious problem for the British army. It was caused by standing in soaking wet, cold socks and boots for prolonged periods, which made the feet swell and go numb, the skin peel off and led, in the worst cases, to gangrene and amputation. To combat the problem, whale oil and anti-frostbite grease were supplied and the men, in pairs, were instructed to use it to massage their feet at least once a day. In addition, new, dry socks were provided so they could change three times a day. However, with the conditions they were facing, this was an inadequate solution and despite regular foot inspections, the problem persisted, with more and more men going sick. Eventually gum-boots were supplied to those in the most exposed positions, which for Ralph did 'excellent service'.

The Battalion was eventually relieved on 12th November after 16 days in the line, living without shelter in mud and water. Nearly 200 men (about twenty per cent of the Battalion strength) had been evacuated due to trench foot and rheumatism, far outnumbering casualties from the 'persistent' enemy fire, which amounted to three killed and eighteen wounded.[81] Moving first to Bethune via Sailly la Bourse, and then to St. Hilaire, the Battalion was in rest billets until the end of November. There they found the local population more hospitable than in other areas and, as always, Ralph enjoyed the time spent in billets and exploring the local area. During this three-week period the men were kept busy. As well as cleaning up thoroughly they underwent physical and technical training and took part in daily drill parades. They were also

[80] WSRO RSR MSS/7/11.
[81] WSRO RSR MSS/7/11; Rutter [n.d.]: 43-44.

Ralph Ellis, Self Portrait

fitted out with vests, leather jerkins, waterproof capes and mitts, to give some protection against the elements.[82]

On 21st November Ralph was promoted to the rank of Sergeant. Perhaps because of this he was selected to return to the front line for seven days' training with the 2nd Batt. Grenadier Guards, the battalion Winston Churchill was attached to at that time. After nearly five months either in, or in close proximity to, the front line, Ralph was not overly enthusiastic about spending the rest period in this way. However, he found the experience interesting; the Guards were picked for their fitness and they set a high standard of discipline, which gave them a feeling of superiority of which they were proud.

At the beginning of December the Battalion moved into reserve at the hamlet of Hingette, near Hinges, and then, on the 11th December into front line trenches in the area of Festubert and Givenchy. Here, as in so much of Northern France and Flanders, the ground was low-lying and extremely wet. The front line – which was the Old British Line – was a series of 'islands' each held by between six and twenty-four men, depending on the size, with the parapet standing above the surrounding mud and water. Support for the men was impossible and they were relieved every 48 hours.[83]

They remained in this sector for the rest of December, moving between the front line, support and reserve and undertaking many exhausting fatigues and working parties. According to Ralph the Battalion seized an opportunity to celebrate Christmas early, and a very enjoyable occasion it was too – 'a cheery evening' with good food, drink and merriment.[84] However, it was soon back to reality and they were back in trenches at Givenchy on the 23rd, enduring a seemingly endless 48 hours of mud and filthy water, under fire from German rifle grenades and mines. Although they were relieved on 25th December, they were disappointed that the transport did not greet them with parcels from home and their packs and greatcoats, so it was a rather cheerless Christmas Day.

The final days of 2015 were spent in the line, facing more mining activity from the Germans, but the first few days of 2016 were spent in rest. On 4th January the 7th Royal Sussex moved into front line trenches in Festubert, the 'islands' or 'grouse butts' brimming with water, mud and rats. But even here Ralph finds a positive angle, describing how billets in the ruined village in the support line offered a little comfort and cosiness to his platoon.

According to the Battalion War Diary, on 13th January the Battalion moved out of the line and eventually arrived in Ham-en-Artois for a period of rest. As well as the usual drills, training, parades and inspections, Ralph spent time drawing and sketching the

[82] WSRO RSR MSS/7/11.
[83] Ibid.
[84] WSRO Add. Mss. 25004: 79.

local area. They were there until 12th February when they took over trenches in the front line opposite the Hohenzollern Redoubt – returning to the sector where they had spent an extremely unpleasant time the previous autumn and where they were to stay for a further two and a half months. According to the Regimental History this was to prove the severest ordeal the battalion had yet faced.[85]

In Volume III of Ralph's memoir the visual images again include sketches and drawings of buildings observed when behind the lines and of his comrades in rest. However, in this volume there are also watercolours showing views of the landscape; some of these are behind the lines, but some show views across the battlefield, an unusual perspective for an infantryman. As his experience of trench warfare increased, Ralph attempted to capture what he saw – and in his emerging role as an observer, his artistic skills were put to good use. But when he came to record his experiences in his memoir, images were not enough; in this volume he increasingly uses words to record what he saw, heard and smelled and he reflected on how he felt.

Towards the end of the volume Ralph's impressions focus in some detail on various aspects of trench warfare in the Vermelles sector opposite the Hohenzollern Redoubt, where the Battalion served for much of the autumn and winter of 1915 and to which they returned in February 1916. A comparison with the Battalion War Diary suggests that these impressions are not chronological and events are confused and conflated to create an overall picture rather than a sequential account, which has the advantage of complementing the official record. In the passage entitled 'The Quarry' he vividly describes the scene at Battalion Headquarters, the dugouts, the advanced dressing station, the trench stores, the men coming and going and the graves amidst the mud and filth. He paints the scene, but this time with words.[86]

Every sector of the Western Front was different, and a range of tactics and weapons were deployed to suit local conditions. In the Vermelles sector, due to the proximity of the opposing front lines, mining was prevalent. Sappers from the Royal Engineers, many of whom were former colliers, dug galleries of varying depths into no man's land and laid massive explosive charges. As both sides were engaged in the activity, in close proximity underground, it was often a race to see who could explode their mines first. The resulting craters were fought over bitterly, using all weapons available including hand-to-hand combat, and eventually occupied by troops, becoming incorporated into the front line. Ralph's detailed observations of one such engagement are related in 'Craters'.[87]

The final passage in Volume III, 'The Observation Posts', recalls an unspecified five-week period Ralph spent visiting all the observation posts in the 12th Division, to which

[85] Rutter [n.d.]: 54.
[86] WSRO Add. Mss. 25004: 95.
[87] WSRO Add. Mss. 25004: 98.

the Battalion was attached. As well as his interesting descriptions of the different 'O.Pips' – for the infantry in the forward lines and for the artillery further back – he gives details about the old farmhouse where he was billeted and the characters he met during the course of his duty. Most obvious in the text is his enjoyment of this job, which gave him freedom to move about; he slept in a safe and comfortable billet at night and he met interesting people. He even spent a day in Bethune, on market day, which gave him a taste of normal life, remote from war.[88] Ralph the soldier had found a role that he enjoyed and that put his artistic talents to good use, for the benefit of the war effort.

[88] WSRO Add. Mss. 25004: 102-104.

Going up to the Line at Loos.

We paraded in the morning and were told that we were to have the honour of relieving a battalion of the Guards that night.

An hour before dusk we were ready to march off and not till then did we regret so much leaving a comfortable billet for all billets are comfortable when it comes to leaving them and marching out into the night.

The sky was cold and grey with a belt of light stretching across the western horizon as we left the last house of the village and swung out on to the track that led across what appeared to be a level plain opening out before us. To the right, a mounted patrol galloped away; and gun limbers loaded with fresh supplies for the guns, left the transport lines which spread out, a ragged encampment on either side of the track and made away swiftly across country into the gathering gloom. The brightly burning fires before the little bivouacs of the transport men looked very inviting and we envied these men who came no further towards the line and slept regular hours of sleep.

The track led us on past a huge black slag heap, then darkness met us, enveloped us and a drizzly rain soaked us through as we stumbled along the uneven way, thick in mud with deep cart tracks to trip our feet. Our equipment, for we are carrying full pack and blanket grows heavier with every step, our surroundings loose all interest, it is ground to be got over, somehow, yet as we march on and on the "very" lights shooting up into the night, then holding still and burning brightly for a while, become like will 'o the wisps, we come no nearer to them.

A cluster of shell wrecked buildings is reached, a dumping ground, engineers with horses and G.S waggons have possession of the track and are making feverish efforts to be rid of their task and get away back, for the Hun knows this spot quite well, a little further on there is the mark of his regard for it littering the way, the bodies of fine transport horses seeming larger in death than in life, lie sprawled out across the muddy track and a smashed waggon adds to the confusion. The transport moves about, the horses pulling and straining to turn the heavy mud clogged wheels; we are only the Infantry and are pressed to the side where the mud and filth is thickest, we can only curse and stumble out of the way, for a minute or two it is a chaos of men pushing together, rifles and packs, plunging horses, curses, mud, deep blackness round about and the persistent rain the only thing that speaks of order and method and one hates it because it is so persistent and so gentle. A man cries out, the deep darkness on our right hides a deep midden of foul water and mud, we pull him out and our nostrils are violated too with the apalling stench he has stirred up and carries with him as we are pushed forward by the men in rear.

Further on a guide for each platoon awaits us and leads us across the open country and the way becomes increasingly difficult, for the chalky ground slips away from under our tired feet with every step we take; shall we ever reach the cursed trenches or are we walking and stumbling in another world out beyond the confines of civilisation, everything is vile, horrible and hateful, we pass a cluster of mud covered rifles and two or three dead collected together for burial, this is our first experience of a battlefield and one wonders if all this weary struggling march is to end in a hunched up, filthy, lifeless body such as these, of far less account now than the rifles that have been collected for further use. Deep strong trenches are crossed and tangles of rusted wire, so that we wonder why the Hun ever left them, so little damaged they look.

Our bit of trench at last and it has taken us at least six hours to reach it, it might have been six days and the trench? Very narrow and about four feet deep, the Guards--men have scooped out little hollow places in the chalk sides, they move out of them stiff and shivering with the damp cold, complaining too of having been there four days, whilst we are shepherded up and down the ragged trench, the sides of which pull and tug at clothing and equipment until we eventually find our appointed place and the relief is completed.

In the line at Loos

A first impression of something that is new always remains most vivid in the mind and subsequent repetitions of the same experience adds little to that first impression and takes nothing away and we gained many first real impressions of warfare during those seven days spent in the line between Hulüch and Loos, of its callous cruelty, waste, and a little of its hardships.

Shells were plentiful as shelling went in those days and on that first morning the chalk flew and stretcher bearers were in great demand, so that we had to move from that bit of trench, then came the task of digging the new front line away out in front and with half a dozen men occupying a section of it during the long day, the trench then about three feet deep so that we had to sit or lie down the whole time and not even smoke, but one gathered the impression that the Hun was quite as busily engaged organising his defences, concentrating upon it and when he had finished would pay more attention to us, he seemed to admit that he

An impression of shells bursting in German front line trench, right of Hulluch.

had been caught napping, had given way much more than he need have done. Winter was approaching and the nights very damp and cold, we shivered many times since then but the cold that grips you on waking after an hours sleep hunched up on the fire-step, takes hold of your whole system and shakes it like a terrier shaking a rat, is always associated with that particular bit of trench.

When the thick white mist gathered about us we left the trench and roamed about over the rough ground clothed with a stubble of dead coarse weeds and grasses, littered too with the implements and apparel of war from the equipment of the infantryman to the battered remains of a couple of our own field guns which had ventured too far forward and the German guns captured and brought back during the night hours, these things were still of value; the dead, the purchase price of this newly gained ground, we buried and the story of their death sometimes was easy to read. There was one group, lying in front of the old German front line which spoke of fierce fighting and brave men, a British officer and three of our men were almost into the deep enemy trench but there lay sprawled out with them two big Prussian soldiers who evidently came out to meet them; so they had died together hot with excitement and hate. We wondered, as two of us reverently buried the leg of a highlander, whether its owner were yet alive, it was a great and wonderful limb, clean and full of strength, there were many parts to be buried, a right arm; and here a hand, clean amputations lying amongst the grass with not another sign of those to whom they belonged.

Hulluch lay in the hollow, broad belts of brown wire entanglements bordered it on the right, where the hill sloped gently up to the ridge, so often crowned with sudden bursts of smoke from our 5.9's. Our men in the first advance had passed over that ridge and seen the country stretching away beyond, few returned, for none came to support them and there must have been many whose remains lay quietly resting in the tall grass.

Yet far worse than that, for half way up, a flutter of white and looking through strong glasses one sees a figure move, then raising himself with evidently great effort, into a half kneeling position and waving for a minute the white flutter of a rag, then all strength and effort gone, dropping suddenly into the cover of grass, he moves again, crawling a few paces, again the feeble waving of the white rag, many would try to get him in, but he is behind the Hun line, others have attempted before with fatal results, there is no definite direction in his movements, Is he blinded? How has he existed for the last seven days since the attack?

No other incident of War could speak more forcibly of its brutality, there is no civilisation, it has been swept away and we have reverted back with a bound to a worse than savage state, and those seven days opened our eyes, the romance of War went out with the sight of these things.

Coming from the Line.

The relief came and we made our way back, as we had come, over the open ground in the darkness, but with the thought of billets in our mind, somewhere to rest and sleep and to be away from the guns which in these seven days had robbed us of more men than we had lost in the two months in the line at Armentieres.

The platoon had passed the old "Lone Tree" which stood up on the plain like an old sentinel, a guide to all the men who came up and down to the line, the only land mark in all that waste of land.

We slipped and stumbled along the greasy foot track in single file, at a very slow pace, for some were almost too tired, too much in need of sleep to make any effort, it is only the thought of what is before and what they are leaving that keeps them going. To one of them that thought is very great, to him the terror of it all has been ever present, never leaving him for a moment, he has been warned for duties with his comrades where the danger to him, has seemed to be greater, a listening post, or a patrol, at such times he has come and begged to be relieved of such work, his intense distress is so apparent that somehow or other one must find him another job, yet his comrades are fond of him, for otherwise he is a good fellow and works well in the doubtful security of a trench, but even then with ever a look for what might happen.

He was almost the last man of the file, wending our way back near to the road and his heart was lifting at the thought of getting away from those things that put so much fear into him, when a little stray bullet, almost spent from its long swift flight, picked him out for a resting place and gave him greater peace.

The road is reached and here we fling off our heavy packs for a while and wait for the other platoons of the Company to join us. Across the way and near to the road is a battery of Field Guns, a blurr of darker shapes in the prevailing darkness and from somewhere near a monotonous voice like a man crying wares, without interest, his thoughts are doubtless far from here, and he cries. "Prepare for Salvo". "Salvo". "Fire". The four guns speak together, so it continues with even regularity and we are not sorry to move on and put a greater distance between us and this noise that irritates nerves already severely tried.

We come to the next halting place where the Battalion will form up and Ye gods! the cookers are here, we see the little bright red spots from their fires and know that hot tea awaits us, after this we fling ourselves down by the roadside our equipment for a pillow and are sound asleep in a moment, to be awakened it seems in 5 minutes time, but the light of another day is with us, then breakfast and we feel that we have almost shaken off the obsession of trench weariness and uncertainty and are free once more to enjoy the earth and that great expanse of glorious sky all about us, with this better feeling we "fall in" and step out, the drums ahead to help us lift our feet on the rough march back to billets.

In succeeding days, we came to know this part of the country well, never going back into the same bit of trench and seldom to the same billets.

When the **second** attack took place at Hulluch, for which we had in part prepared the night before, by digging the assembly trench; our Brigade were in reserve and the Battalion was crowded into the big lofts above the stables and cowsheds of the large farm at Noyelles. From the bank of ground rising higher above the village; where the road runs to Vermelles, we watched the smoke and gas clouds going over and the bursting shrapnel above, it looked rather insignificant, in the distance, against the majesty and expanse of cloud and sky. We were ready but not required just then.

It was after; and whilst walking on the main road from Bethune to Loos, just beyond Noyelles, the road dips down, then rises again to Mazingarbe; and the ground on either side is scarred by old trenches, shell holes, bits of wire entanglements; and away towards Vermelles, were the guns, still barking, like dogs excited after a fight.

It was early morning; and here and there, caught up on the snags of wire, on the tall stems of withered grass; were many fine white threads, just as one has seen the fine cobwebs, in the woods in autumn, covered with gems of dew, that stretch across the little pathways.

.. Desolation. ..

On the fourth night came orders, that our Company should take up wire entanglements and place them before the Trench, in the narrow strip of no-mans-land.

A fatigue to remember.

The entanglements made by engineers?, were supposed to be collapseable so that it would be possible to carry them along a trench, one collapsed altogether, the framework of the others was made of heavy Timber, firmly fixed together and a mass of barbed wire curling about it, appalling things for two men to carry over smooth ground; but a task to baffle super-men, over the way we had to travel.

The road seemed to be the right border of that storm, we on the right had experienced comparitively calm days, thinking little of the shells that burst away to the left. Before we had returned from our task, we had found how near one may be to such activity and know scarcely anything of it.

Our way at first, lay across the open and in the darkness the ground appeared as desolate as could be, no place for a living thing; and everything to trip the feet of the carrying men, whilst here and there were our dead unburied, old trenches battered out to a great width, to be bridged; slow progress, but at last we reach a point where it is not safe to continue over the top; and we must get into the trench, it is then our real difficulties begin, the trench turns and twists, it was difficult enough to get into it, with these cumbersome abortions, that catch in everything, pull half the parapet down and tear the clothes and hands of those trying their best to manage them, they work with a will and we continue by degrees along the trench, it is an arduous, almost impossible labour, every step of the way. A long narrow part of trench utterly stops further progress and we must try over the top again. The very lights, not far ahead are continually going up, by their light the Hun may have seen the first few making their way forward. Suddenly, riffle and machine guns crack and rattle, sending the bullets hissing about us, everyone is back into the trench, whilst two men with their entanglement just breasting the parapet, drop it suddenly, the lower man lying flat with the mass of wire above him, like a sparrow caught in a sieve trap.

Just at this spot, the trench has been blown wide by a shell during the day; and a man resting by the side, rises quickly and moves to a few feet away, having suddenly discovered

.. Remains of small wood near Vermelles. ..

that he has been almost sitting on the severed head of a man, the trunk was with another just beyond the parapet, while one body rests just beneath the soil at our feet, the men dwelling in the trench have made attempts to dig; they are new to such things and cry out the warning to those who pass, not to tread just there. I watch; it is impossible, they all receive the warning too soon, or too late and step on the very spot.

The commotion ahead increases and consequently the jumpiness of those whose business it is to hold the line, such alarms have come frequently during the past four days. Bombers to re-inforce go by, Middlesex men, [Die-hards] – who spit out to us in passing, highly coloured expletives, descriptive of the Hun and their own die-hardedness; but they are full of pluck and push up the trench with as much vigour as though it led to a boxing match or the canteen. Then back come the orders, carried from mouth to mouth. "More bombs wanted, ammunition, very lights"; and so we hand them up from one to the other, until the cry for more ceases and we wait, expecting the next order to be for men.

It quietens a little, the night is well advanced, so the entanglements are left to adorn the parapet, as the order comes down to "Clear out".

What has happened ahead ?.

Of all our bombers whom we sent to re-inforce, none came back, all were casualties. Many months after, one told me of an incident that took place there. He was one of three splendid fellows and great pals. Another attack was expected and the trench was full of men, waiting. It grew quieter, oppressively so and few lights went up. Then, three of the sentries peering forward, trying to see what the darkness held, fell back into the trench, dead, shot through the head; and immediately, came bombs, spinning and bursting into the trench, striking down the men with bomb in hand, waiting to throw; these dropping from their hand with pin released, added to the dreadful chaos. One of the three was hit, in the stomach, remaining fully conscious and suffering great agony, so that he begged of his great pal to shoot him; and he was about to do so, but a lad, a lance-corporal, clung to him beseeching him not to; then fate stepped in with a bomb and killed the two, to leave the other with his agony. It was rumoured that he was eventually got away, out of that hell, still conscious and carried screaming with pain, as some _must_. down that broken trench. The point was settled a long time after, when resting near a Casualty Clearing Station; and walking through the British Cemetry, found his name on one of the little white crosses, of the many that were here to the memory of men, died of wounds. In such ways did we loose the best of our men, but the trench was held and handed over the following night as a thriving concern.

.. Rest ..

In November 1915, the Division finally came out of the line to the rest area round about Lillers, the Battalion occupying billets in St Hilaire, a village east of Lillers.
To rest, for however short a time, and we remained here for about 3 weeks, always includes a certain amount of training to be carried out daily, new "stunts" to be practised; and for some of the Officers and N.C.O's special courses of training to undergo, one expected that, but not to be sent for such training, back into the front line after nearly five months, either in, or in close proximity to it; yet one Officer and N.C.O. must go and see how the Guards behave when in the line.

We did not know they were there, except for very special occasions, we thought of them enjoying life round about St Omer. But evening found us, attached to B. Company of the 2nd Batt. Grenadier Guards in the front line at Rouge Croix. The Platoon Sergt was a good fellow and the seven days passed well and with some interest, one saw that the men were picked for fitness generally, and they set a stan--dard for discipline, which the men must often have found most irksome, but then it gave them a sound feeling of superiority, of which they were proud.
At that time Winston Churchill was attached to this Battalion of the Guards, his chief occupation appeared to be in attempting to keep pace with a most energetic and vigilant company commander who had eyes to see all things on his way through the trench, while Major Churchill 10 paces in rear, or thereabouts, tried to maintain an interesting conversation.

A Battalion H.Q. of the 2nd Grenadiers. Winston Churchill's billet, Rouge Croix.

.. Canal at Hinges. ..

Hinges and Givenchy

S! Hilaire was left and we marched again towards the line, staying for a few days at Hinges, a very small village. A canal divided it, on which the large hospital barges glided quietly by, a smooth, even way of travel for the wounded.

Bethune was quite near, a half hours' walk along the canal bank; and it was good to get to a large town again, its cake shops provided a feast of sweetness undreamed of.

There were other things to be done during those few days, before taking over trenches at Givenchy, fatigues, that robbed us of good nights rest, the most precious gift of the time spent out of the line.

Practically the whole of the Battalion were required, to carry up, gas cylinders, into the front line at Givenchy. Motor lorries hastened us nearer to a certain point. Then the work began, a pole between two men, on which the cylinders were slung and carried on their shoulders, not too hard a task; but before we reached the trench, — we avoided much of the long and winding communication trenches, — we came to a length of road, where to the right, the ground was fairly level and exposed to the Hun, just the place to tempt a Machine gunner to occasionally sweep with bullets; and they came, little unseen furies.

Now a cylinder full of poison gas, is'nt a thing you care about dropping suddenly on a hard road, it might crack and then annoy you, neither is it sensible to remain upright on a road swept by bullets.

The cylinders were lowered to earth most carefully, but they lowered themselves to cover with greater speed, remaining there until the shower had passed.

On the way back through the trench, one was startled to run into a sailor, standing, stolidly looking out over the parapet, for a moment, one forgot the trench and almost felt the roll of a boat, and followed the direction in which he looked, to see if the great waters lay out there. We talked for a minute while the files in rear caught up. No, he did not think much of it, too much mud and dirt generally, he much preferred the ways of the sea and the order and the cleanliness of ships, but was glad to have seen these things.

. . Christmas . 1915 . .

Christmas was almost with us, before we left Hinges for the line again; and in some way we had to celebrate, as best we could, in such a place, the Officers were of that opinion and gave freely.

The Dining Hall was an old cart shed, which we hung about with tarpaulins and sacking, borrowed from the transport, it kept out most of the cold, rain laden wind. A dimly lighted place, filled with the faces of men, all else seemed to melt away into the shadows; and the faces talked, talked freely without restraint and fed and drank sumptuously of the good fare provided, for the cooks had excelled themselves; and when you have tasted nothing but stew or bully beef, day after day; roast pork with a liberal supply of fresh vegetables is vastly appreciated, of course the feast did not end with that, there were a lot of etcæteras and drinks to be disposed of, which seemed rather, to put the soloists off song, but the choruses, sung in mass, almost raised the roof and brought the little kiddies of the farm running wide and wonder eyed to the door. It was a cheery evening.

. . Givenchy . .

It was no great march to Givenchy, flat country that seemed in many places to be below the level of the canals that intersected it, and it was along the bordering road of one we marched for a mile, a platoon at a time and there was one platoon of the Brigade that was very unfortunate.

Away to the right, beyond the waste of uncultivated fields and hidden somewhere

. . Marshy ground . Festubert. . .

midst the broken belt of trees, lay a battery of our heavies; and the Hun gunners were sending over in a methodical way, shells, that searched, here and there, up and down those meadows, trying to find our gun-pits. As this platoon passed the line of fire, one screeching shell, came to earth, very short of its intended target and right into their midst, so that, that Battalion went up to the line minus one platoon.

We occupied trenches, where the village had been, on a slight rise of ground, they wound about the heaps of brick, and jagged spurs of wall, haunted by one or two half wild cats, who still made this their home.

Time is a vacancy to be filled, and the life with which it is filled, shortens or lengthens it out of all proportion to any preconceived idea of what is a certain area of time; for instance, 48 hours when thought of in the matter of leave, well, it is very short, but 48 hours, to be spent in bad trenches, impresses the mind with a totally different and far longer spread of life-time, there is no comparison.

48 hours at a time, was quite long enough at Givenchy. The whole place from the support line to No-mans-land, was a sea of mud and the trenches, might have been gullies formed by the rain, in some places their walls, a slithering mass of slimy mud, almost mer, trench boards floated on the filthy water that here and there almost reached to a mans waist.

The war was carried on chiefly through the medium of rifle grenades and mines, for all parts of the line had their specialities, the former could be seen and heard approaching, but not always avoided, the latter, came suddenly, with a burst of shrapnel, timed to burst about the ground at the same moment; and catch exposed men on the fringe of the mine. It made the ground to rock, the rotting trenches to come tumbling in, burying those who existed there, forcing the soft mud into eyes, nose and ears, plastering them with it from head to foot.

But only those who were badly injured could be carried down such trenches, the others must stumble along as best they can, no stretcher can pass through, it must be carried

"Estaminet corner" Festubert.

most of the way, above the heads of the bearers; and it takes hours to get through less than a mile of trench, strenuous, tiring labour for the bearers, and heaven knows what to the wounded.

On Christmas morning we were relieved, going back to the broken houses and farm buildings, just below the ridge, which, although so near, were so little disturbed in those days by shell fire. The day was spent in attempting to clean up, scrape and dry sodden mudded clothing, but the transport disappointed us, as they brought us neither parcels, with which we had hoped to make the day cheery ~~with~~, or our packs, ~~is~~ where rested our great-coats. However it was a little more comfortable, sleeping under cover, than on a wet fire-step, with our feet dangling in mud and water, and when it came to marching back in two days time, to Hinges once more, we were not sorry to be without packs.

.. Festubert ..

The line we occupied at Festubert, was just beyond the village and to the north of Givenchy; on low ground, that in those winter months, formed a swamp of mud and water. The front line consisted of, a series of posts; islands or grouse-butts they were called, the first name most accurately described them, the trench that had formed the connection was brimming over with water, sheets of water spread out like miniature lakes in no-mans-land and all approaches led through mud, of varying depth and consistency.

Having once arrived at your post, there you had to remain, until night came again and under cover of darkness, other posts could be visited, by scrambling along the crumb--ling breastwork. We attempted a fire, but the damp wood, smoked, and attracted the Hun gunners, who with. H.E. shells, sent the mud and water flying skywards; and made us ~~,~~ desert our six square feet of fairly dry soil, with its low sand-bagged roof, and spread out along the trench waist deep in water. As the day crept up over that waste of flooded land, a few Huns could be seen scrambling hastily along their parapet; and we knew that they too were in similar plight, but one paid the penalty of not taking cover earlier.

The support line was much better, the big breastwork of sand-bags and soil, gave cover for movement during the day; but old trenches, low ground and shell holes, water filled, made a ready bath for those who walked clumsily along the narrow trench boards, as some did, when coming in at night, disappearing suddenly and rising, spluttering, full of panic at such a sudden immersion in ice cold, unseen waters.

Rats, black and brown and of all sizes, lived here in great numbers, it was not uncommon when about to enter one of the low, wet shelters built against the breast-works; to be met by three or four of them, leisurely trotting out in single file, and such places, looked more suited to their needs than ours; they were too fat and lazy to get out of your way, when walking along the slats at night and could be kicked out into the black water on either side.

There is one great advantage in winter, in living in a deserted village such as Festubert; where one Battalion at least remained in support; and that, is for the almost unlimited quantity of fire-wood to be obtained. There were two billets we occupied at different times, mere husks of buildings, the broken walls sand-bagged and made warm and snug with a fire that seldom burnt out; and around these the men gathered, talked, giving an insight into how past days had been spent, one, keen, reliable man, spoke of many happy poaching days in Sussex, while another an under-keeper gave the opposite side of the picture; and one untidy scamp speaking of "home" life and days spent at a reformatory school, made one wonder, that he had turned out as well as he had.

These were vagabond days, too few in number, when one could find time to wander out into the swampy deserted meadows, overgrown with tall rushes and coarse grass, giving cover

Canal near Givenchy.

to coot and moorhen, seeking to disturb the bittern we believed to be there, or other interesting wild fowl; and then to return, to a dim lit building, a blazing wood fire and to revel in sleep, curled up in a snug blanket.
No 9 Platoon was fortunate in billets at Festubert.

Entrance to Chateau. Ham-en-artois.

Ham - en - artois.

About February 1916, we moved back to Ham for a short rest. We liked this village, thoroughly enjoying the time spent there, which culminated in a few days divisional training in moving from place to place.

The entrance to the Chateau, which had at one time been connected with the Church near by, was odd and interesting. The latter bearing the date 1689, but all the interest existed in the exterior of the buildings, the interior had been spoilt, the decoration of the church being of the tawdriest possible. The Chateau was used as a Battalion Headquarters.

.. The Church at Ham. ..

The Vermelles Sector.

Again we returned to the sector between Cambrai and Hulluch, a spot we were least likely to forget. We had not forgotten our experiences there about the end of October and In the early days of November 1915, our first visit to the Hohenzollern Redoubt.
We were to have "gone over", straightened out a bit of line after the attack at Loos.

Hid discreetly behind a big slag heap near to Noyelles, two lines of trenches had been dug, they represented our own front line, and "Little Willy", the german trench to be attacked. For two wet and very cold days, we practised the "stunt", going over the ground again and again, until every man knew his job and exactly what was expected of him, we were lectured about it too and resented greatly the manner in which it was put to us,, "The trench would be very easy to attack and capture, it was very lightly held, by about two men and a boy". These were the sort of words wasted upon us. Nothing was gained by a ridiculous under-estimation of a task, which we were there to do irrespective of what it might cost. we could treat the thing humourously in our own way, but objected to being treated like children, expected to believe implicitly such lightly spoken words, no appeal was made to the finest qualities in the men.
A more depressing beginning to an attack could not have been than on the night we went up to take over trenches. Heavy rain swept down in torrents, so that long before we reached the trenches, we were wet through; yet the men, knowing what was before, marched off singing lustily "The last boats leaving for home".
The support line, in which we first "put up", was in places knee deep in water and the first night was spent, sitting on the fire-step, with waterproof sheets hung over a bit of the trench, making a very inadequate protection against the unceasing rain. The communication trenches up to the front line were either feet deep in water or mud, thick and thin. During the sixteen days spent in the line, four only were spent in the support trench, where our work consisted of fatigues, attempting to clear trenches,

Sketch from Hohenzollern Redoubt looking towards "Tower Bridge"

carrying up bombs etc. but the rain beat down incessantly, making the little landslides in the trenches, forming quagmires of mud and this was before the issue of gum boots. A few N.C.O's were detailed to reconnoitre the position to be attacked, and, taking a hasty look over the parapet in several places, saw, a line of our own dead, before the enemy trench, "Jocks" they were, cut down in an even row, as they had advanced; they at least had met with greater resistance than two men and a boy !.

The attack became impossible, the men were too unfit and the ground and weather too unfavourable, each day a greater number of men from the Brigade, went back, suffering from trench feet and rheumatism, hobbling back, feet swathed in sand-bags, getting along on their knees or on the backs of men from the R.A.M.C. down the deserted rail-road to Vermelles. Head Quarters became rampage over this, gum boots arrived and excellent service they rendered too, also a Staff Officer paid us a hurried visit, making theoretical suggestions, on how to avoid trench feet, one scheme was to reserve a part of the trench, where men must go two at a time, at least once a day and rub each others feet with grease, and so it was neatly labelled, according to orders. "This bay is reserved for the greasing and rubbing of feet". Then someone with feeling and humour, posted a notice on either side of the next fire-bay, which read. "This bay is reserved for wailing, and gnashing of teeth."

Each day we expected to be relieved, but the days passed by, a very few fine and the nights seemed always wet. The men stuck it splendidly, although during the last few days, they were doing sentry duty at the rate of two hours on and two off, also working to improve the trench and left it with trench boards down in a far better condition than we found it. One cannot help speaking of ones own section, who worked together so well, one man whose age was 41 or 42, made himself responsible for the cooking, although he could not be spared from sentry duty, always had a bit of fire going, in spite of rain, [we lived on the firestep

Periscope sketch from the Redoubt, shewing "Little Willy", the front line German Trench and the line of our dead in front.

                                    Flowers o' the field
                                    They are gathered;
                                    Withered away:
                                    But die not.

with no other shelter than a waterproof sheet will provide], and provided hot tea regularly for the whole section three times a day, watching over too what cooking could be done. It may not sound very much in the telling, but under these conditions and at the same time, to keep cheery and good tempered as they all did, speaks of a very high moral, This man did not report sick until he was quite ill and almost unable to move with rheumatism, another, warned for sentry duty at night, while the rain was pouring down, did his best to get up on to the fire step, it was impossible, too ill, with limbs badly swollen, even their faces swelled and it was with great difficulty that he was got away that morning, being quite unable to walk through the mud clogged trenches; these are details which give an idea of the spirit of the men; there was not another man to take his place who had not just come off sentry, so a hard worked stretcher bearer volunteered to do the two hours in the drenching rain, peering out into the blackness, broken occasionally by Bosch very lights that spluttered quickly to earth, made visible for a moment the drifting rain and the vague shapes of the dead, that, to the tired brain, were like crouching figures creeping silently forward.

Then came orders to proceed to Sailly-Labourse billeting, the news leapt from mouth to mouth down the trench.

The following day the Battalion came out and neither before nor since has one seen men in such a condition, they marched into billets very slowly, mud covering them from head to foot.

The Vermelles sector could not be called a "soft" part of the line, but in returning to it, we knew that fairly good times could be had, whilst in reserve, when the Brigade would be billeted, part in reserve and part in villages near to the Town, in which the people seemed more hospitable than we found them to be, in the poorer villages we came to, later on in the Somme district and on other parts of the line. At some of the farms and houses they would insist on the men coming into the large living room, in the evening, or as soon as the parades for the day had finished and made them feel perfectly free and easy to do as they pleased, write their home letters, play at cards and more often, finish the evening with an impromptu concert. On wet winter evenings, this added considerably to the comfort of the few days spent in reserve before returning again to the line.

In Bethune the billet was always a large school or factory, holding from one to two Battalions of men.

It was not a long march from that place to the line, along the straight, tree bordered road that led on further to Loos, always bearing up and down on its rough cobbled surface the traffic of war and a few civilian vehicles too that came as far as Mazingarbe where a few French people still hung on to wrecks of houses, making a living by selling café, bread, chocolate and oranges to passing troops. Here traffic by day ceased, the road went on alone, until it met the traffic of the Huns beyond Loos.

Only a few hours march and one could leave the busy streets, full of life and colour; and be transfered to another world, a sombre, pitiless world of filth, death and decay; and when dwelling in the one, the other was as far away as a distant country, set beyond the far seas.

Of this sector, one might best portray it, by attempting to describe a few impressions that forced themselves most easily on the memory.

.. The Quarry ..

From the outskirts of Vermelles, hid between the ruined dwellings, began the deeply cut, long communication trenches, that a little further on crossed the railway line, passed through jutting fragments of brickwork, a few splintered stumps of trees and then zig-zagged through bare, barren country, for in these winter days, nature seemed to have deserted it entirely, giving it up to the foul, destroying devices of man; then; more than half way up, the trench seemed suddenly to cease, in reality it dipped steeply down, but to the newcomer, who came, toiling up the long trench and then to be faced suddenly with open ground before him, made him fear for a moment that he had taken the wrong way, which had pitched him helplessly into no-mans-land. This was known as the Quarry and we sometimes wondered why it should take its name from old associations, when present ones might have suggested something much more descriptive. Thick chalky mud covered its surface, filled the shell holes and shallow trench that crossed it, where men passing through, floundered and cursed the thick mass that squelched, sucked and dragged at boots and clothing.

Battalion Head quarters was here, with its little following of runners and scouts, a few sappers and the advanced dressing station too, crowded into dug-outs, dug into the bank of the quarry nearest the Hun, where his 4" and 5·9's found a difficulty in reaching, often they came hissing over, but the mud was soft and many men, trying to hurriedly cross that mud-clogged space, owed their lives to the soft mud, for the shells plunged deep down into the unresisting earth, failing to explode.

Not all escaped, close under the right bank were two – three, rows of plain crosses, and often too the still bodies, covered with a sodden blanket, splashed with mud from the feet of passing men; of others, to increase the growth of crosses, that, one day disappeared with the sudden blasting advent of a Hun H.E. shell.

In the open space to the left, dumped there in the mud, were trench stores of sand-bags, wire and stakes; to be taken up and used by men from the front and support lines, who came after "stand down", when the last glimmer of daylight had faded out of the sky, filing out of the further trench, vague shapes in the gathering gloom, sandbags wrapped about their legs and flung across their shoulders, slight protection against rain and mud, dirty and mud-covered, clustering about the dump, stumbling and splashing through the filth, to pick up their alloted load and get away quickly from this open spot, to the shelter of the trench again.

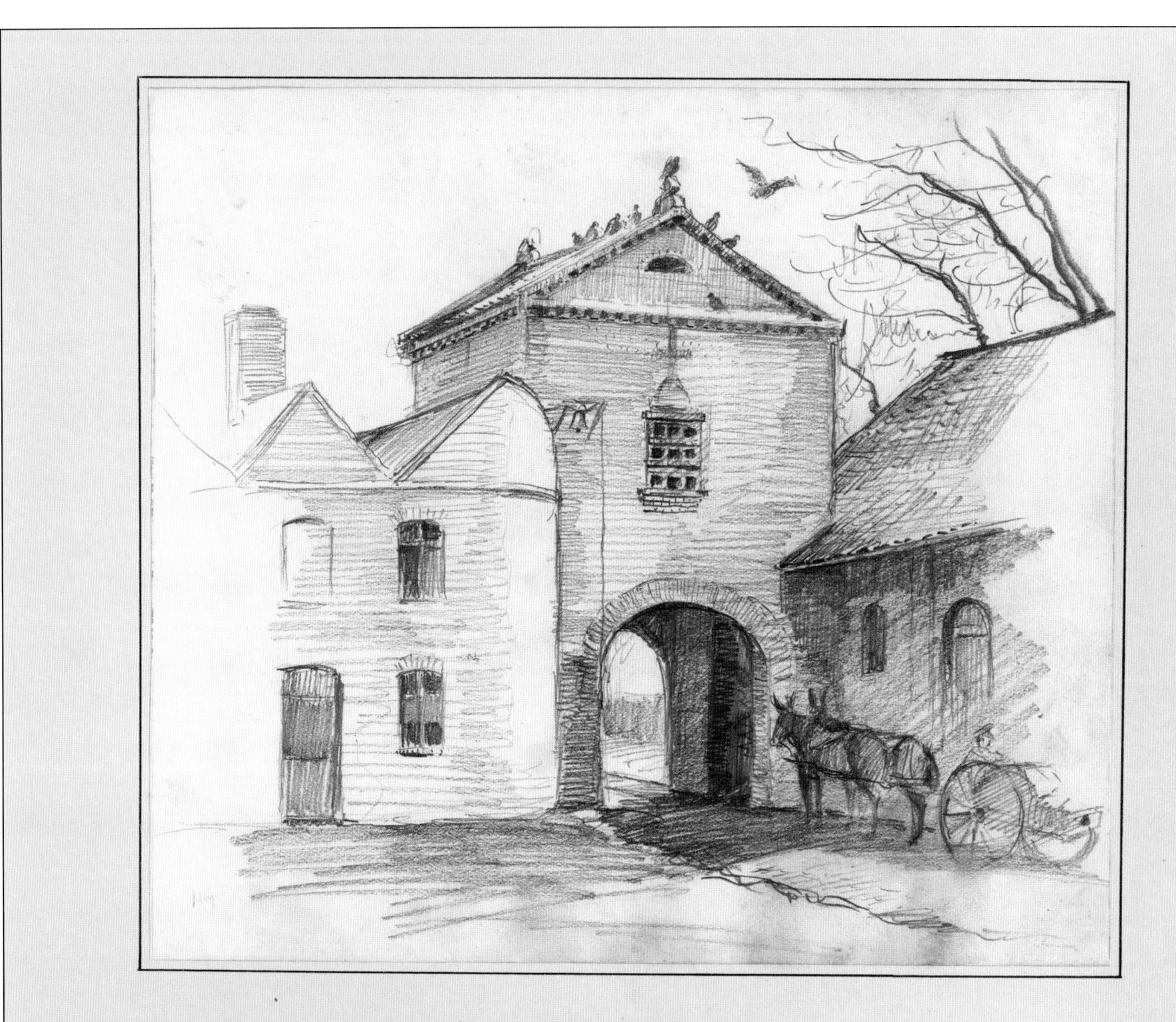

. . Entrance to farm Noyelles. . .

.. Craters. ..

Wherever the lines of the two opposing trenches came within a hundred yards of each other, both sides immediately began to undermine, running out long galleries, elaborate workings of varying depth, carried out by R.E. Sappers, men drawn from all Regiments, many who had previous to the War, worked in the colleries at home, but the fatiguing work of dragging the full sandbags of heavy wet soil or bulky chalk from the head of the working along the dark low tunnel to the entrance of the sap and then away down the trench to some spot as far from the working as possible; was of course the work of the Infantry, without the extra pay. In this Sector mining was most active, as though each, had given up the idea of attacking over ground, but instead, feverishly burrowed forward like moles. During one spell in the line, the average was almost two mines sprung per day on a 1000 yard front. The favourite time being just before or after dawn or sunset.

Whilst in Alexandra trench, our front line to the right of the Hohenzollern Redoubt; and, hearing that a large mine was to "go up" near there at such and such a second, thought it would be interesting to watch for, and chose a position at the head of a Communication trench, lying flat on the high slope of parapet.
Looking back, half left, the ground fell away, but gave no suggestion of its past state of a fertile slope, tilled and clothed in a patchwork of living, ordered vegetation, the ground was dead, bare of any growth, except for a small patch of grey green, between the support lines further back. Trenches, old and new, were many, so many that it was impossible to make out any system, one saw only, varying shades of brown earth, with here and there a streak or patch of white chalk, that became more rugged and broken where the two opposing lines were known to be. The Redoubt, where was it? It looked so well on a map, we knew it was out there somewhere, mixed up in that torn tortured earth, it was hard to believe that hundreds of men faced each other, dwelt amidst that still, lifeless soil.

The seconds slipped by, then, while eyes watched intently, a patch of brown earth rose gently, without haste, as though that breast of ground had just heaved a sigh of resignation, at being so torn and tortured again; the shape of it resembled a mushroom, but rather more oval in shape, this, for a fraction of a second, then, a flash of flame, set amidst upward surging smoke, burst forth and earth and other things soared high into the air, the noise of the explosion rocked the air and even at this distance one felt the ground shake, immediately a pandemonium of noise and hate raged about that spot, much shrapnel burst with a ripping sound, sending out a promise to tear and torture all it came in touch with, machine guns rattled with feverish haste and then came the sound of the burst of the little shrapnel, the hand grenades and they were many; and spoke of men stumbling and bombing their way forward over the broken smoking earth, to claim the crater; In half an hour all is quiet, the crater is ours to hold and to keep!, but keeping craters cannot be recommended as a hobby.

An early idea of some Generals, was, that craters should be held from the inner forward lip and it took them quite a long time to be convinced that this was a stupid waste of valuable men, when, half an hours residence in such a spot would have made a quite convincing argument against such a method; later on, we came to hold them from the outer lip, the crater itself being a no-mans-land.
Our front line brushed the outer lip of some, saps ran out to others; where a man watched continually, with rifle and bomb, ready to hand, staring at a scene, so lifeless, as to seem unreal, even the sky seems shut out, the mind through the seeing eye is gripped at once by the deadness and poignancy of that deep, cone shaped space, and there on the opposite bank of the crater, lies the body of a comrade, just as he had fallen backwards, his head cleaned of hair, flung back and arms stretched out with rifle near, and he lies Oh! so still, nothing moves; so different is the quiet of nature, to the stillness and vacancy of death.

· 4/7/16 ·

The German Front line and Puits S.r Elie from a front line O.Pip.

Entrance to Bosch dug out.

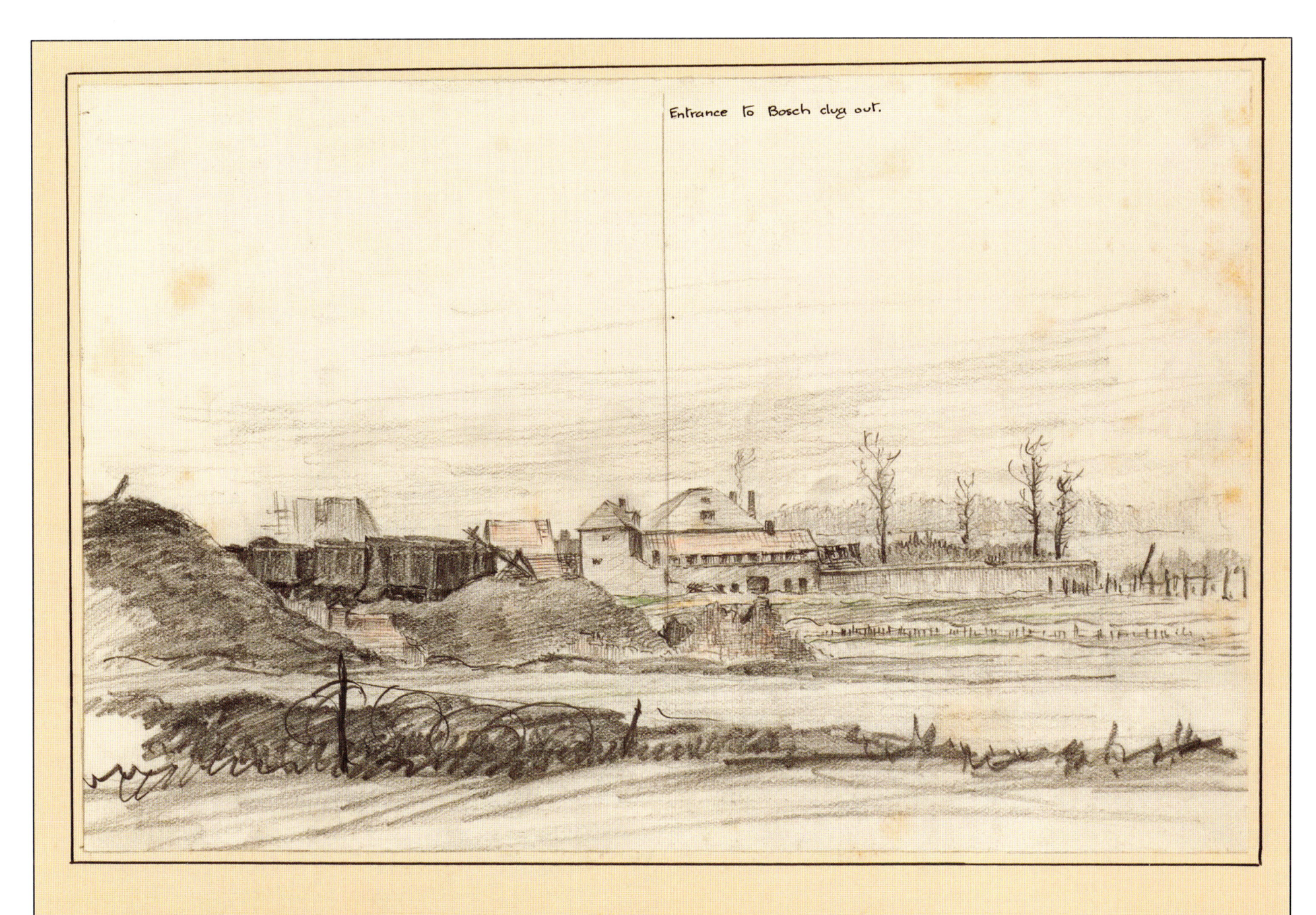

Sketch from O. Pip at Border Redoubt shewing corner of Fosse 8 and 4 lines of German Trenches.

. . The Observation Posts . .

A special job, lasting five weeks, gave one the opportunity of seeing almost all the observation posts in the Divisional area, tramping many miles of trenches during the day, but always returning at night to comfortable quarters, a room in the old farm house at Noyelles. Five weeks that were thoroughly enjoyed, perhaps because of the thought of that undisturbed rest to return to at night.

The farm itself was well built and complete, scarcely damaged at all from shell fire although so near to an "active" part of the line, but almost eighteen months of fair wear and tear from a succession of troops constantly billeted there had not improved the look of the place. The owners, whom it was rumoured were Germans [to account for the preservation of the farm] had long since gone, leaving a few quarrelsome farm hands to look after the place and the small herd of cattle and sheep, that grazed in the fields, pitted with shell holes and divided by belts of wire right up to Vermelles. one poor bedraggled peacock, a remnant of past glories still strutted about the place, uttered discordant cries occasionally and tried to find companionship with the few pigs, the only residents who seemed really to enjoy the disorder and neglect.

The Infantry Observation Posts, were usually the most interesting, being nearer to the enemy, seldom further back than the support line; and one or two in saps running out from the front line, from these well hid places there was often much to be seen.

The Artillery O. Pip's lay a little further back as a general rule, were more commodious places, with a deep dug-out attached, to bolt to in case of necessity, were stronger built, so that it was almost comfortable to sit there and watch for movement, away there in the distance, beyond the network of trenches that scarred the ground in all directions and were so many that they became a maze of brown soil.

Fosse 8, the long low slag heap just within the Bosch lines, was a great feature of this sector, dominating the greater part of it, for observation purposes it must have been splendid, overlooking the ground far behind our lines and from there, machine guns could at night almost fire down into and infilade some of our trenches, no amount of shelling appeared to alter the shape of it. our big H.E. shells would sometimes burst on the top of the slag heap, sending up a cloud of black dust that quickly settled again but left no apparent impression of where it had burst.

Divisional H.Q employed observers for special posts; and these were men who had volunteered for the duty from our cavalry unit, King Edwards Horse. About half a dozen of them lived in an old cellar of what had been the padre's house in Vermelles, going up to the O. Pips during the day and returning at dusk.
They were a splendid set of men, brought together from many parts of the world, a cattle rancher and a railroad inspector from Argentina, an American University man, an English B.A and Entomologist, and one tall boy from Australia, possessing a dark god-like face that any woman must have loved on sight.
It made a fine finish to a day, to walk across the open deserted fields, past a battery of our field guns, carefully camouflaged, just on the outskirts of Vermelles, and drink a dish of tea with them, down in the bricked cellar, lit by one or two candles, stuck on ra bully beef tins, or sitting outside on the bit of grass remaining to the garden and then to listen to the talk for an hour, returning, when darkness had fallen and Vermelles was a hive of activity, with many limbers bringing food for the troops in the line, rumbling through its streets, deep in shadow from the gaunt remains of the houses, whose outter walls still remained standing; fatigue parties came down from the line, clustered for a while at the corner, about the old brewery where hot soup could be had for the asking, then away to the R.E. Dump or the Transport limbers, to go back loaded with rations or material for the defence and up-keep of the trenches.

One other recreation came my way. spending a day in Bethune, market day, when few troops were there, and the big open square, surrounded by old buildings and thriving modern shops, looked down upon masses of life and colour that moved about the many stalls, laden with all manner of farm produce and cheap household goods and hummed with rapid speaking voices, the clatter of horses drawing the high black hooded carts over the stone cobbles. A place as remote from War, as the interior of the big Church, where reigned peace and great quiet, amidst a wonderful wealth of deep rich colouring; and one far window, held glass of a most glorious blue, that cast a haze over stone column and panelled wall, comparable to the blue that nature paints her distant-alluring lands with.

Incidents to remember, walking back too, in the night hours to Noyelles, when the straight road in front ripples away, a pale blue path in a land of mystery; and tired marching men relieved from the line, loom up largely, pass quietly, even the regular tramp of their feet seems silenced in the quiet of the still night.

VOLUME IV

The fourth volume of Ralph Ellis's memoir continues with the movements of the 7th Battalion Royal Sussex Regiment during the spring of 1916. Arriving back in the Hohenzollern/Vermelles sector in mid-February, the battalion found the conditions just as difficult as they had experienced in the autumn. The weather continued to be wet and cold, with flooded trenches, thick mud, snow and slush, but at least they were a little better equipped than they had been in the autumn. They quickly re-established the trench routine of several days in the firing line, in support, in reserve and then a few days in rest, where the hard physical work of training and fatigues continued.

Volume IV continues with Ralph's impressions of the life of an infantryman on the Western Front. Each sector had its own particular character and weapon of choice. As well as mining, in the Hohenzollern/Vermelles sector it was the bombers who were most active and Ralph describes how they operated and existed in 'Bombing Posts'. In the memoir the Germans are usually referred to generically as the 'Bosches', the 'Hun' or 'the enemy', but in this passage a German bomber, 'a cheeky impudent youngster' becomes an individual and is swiftly dispatched. This is one of the few occasions when Ralph talks about the death of an individual. Bodies in no man's land and roadside cemeteries are occasionally mentioned in the text, but even more rarely do they appear in his visual images.[89]

As with many of the incidents recorded in the memoir, it is hard to pinpoint the exact timing of the first action described in the passage entitled 'A Hun Attack'. Throughout March and April there was a great deal of action in this sector: mining, artillery and bombing attacks occurred almost daily at some point in the line. Being in a state of constant expectation of attack put considerable strain on the men. Ralph recalls waiting and watching as the Germans shelled positions around them, fear exacerbated by the imagination. The large shape that swooped overhead, like a symbol of evil and death, was only an owl.[90]

The second attack Ralph describes in this passage is a gas attack when the battalion had just arrived in billets at Annequin at the end of their tour in trenches, so it is out of sequence. Recorded in the Battalion War Diary on 27th April, this attack illustrates the importance of good gas mask discipline. Ralph also notes that the horses and mules, which were unprotected, were set loose to escape the gas. Although there were no casualties among the men, the War Diary states that later that day, after a twelve-mile march, the horses were 'very slack & seemed to have been affected by gas'.[91] This is

---

[89] WSRO Add. Mss. 25005: 117.
[90] WSRO Add. Mss. 25005: 120.
[91] WSRO RSR MSS/7/11; WSRO Add. Mss. 25005: 122.

hardly surprising and is a reminder of the millions of horses and mules that served, suffered and died in the Great War.

Most nights small groups of men were sent out to repair and renew the barbed wire defences in no man's land, a dreaded job captured in another of Ralph's impressions. In the passage entitled 'Wiring' a routine task becomes a living nightmare with a graphic evocation of what the men encountered – and the enemy were the least of their problems. Constant mining and shelling had rendered the ground between the two front lines a morass of mud, shell holes, barbed wire and dead bodies, which had to be negotiated in persistent rain and impenetrable darkness, all within easy range of the German trenches. This was the reality of life in the trenches for an infantryman.

At the beginning of March 1916 the battalion was involved in the heaviest fighting they had yet seen. According to the War Diary, on 2nd March a number of mines were exploded close to the enemy front line and the 8th Royal Fusiliers occupied the newly created front line craters, under heavy shell-fire. The following day the 7th Royal Sussex took over the positions in the front line and then came under an intense bombardment from large Trench Mortars, Howitzers and Field Guns. On the 4th March the Germans continued their bombardment and their bombing parties made many attempts to detrench and counter-attack, all of which were repelled by the 7th Royal Sussex, who retained all the positions they had taken over. This action became known as 'The Battle of the Craters', and the casualties (dead and wounded) sustained by the battalion were nine officers and 210 other ranks.[92]

'C' Company was in the thick of the fighting, but Ralph missed it as he was on leave. Returning very soon afterwards to hear about it and soon to see for himself the aftermath of the battle, he was clearly shocked by what he saw, as he relates in 'Crater Fighting at the Hohenzollern Redoubt'. The recently dead, men he had served and lived with, were very much in evidence and he possibly felt guilty for not being with his men during this terrible time. Despite what they had been through, and the evidence of the high price paid, the survivors were soon cheered by a glimpse of sunshine, a skylark and the promise of food, cigarettes and being relieved. On the 8th March Lieutenant-General Sir Hubert Gough inspected the battalion and addressed all ranks, complimenting them on their defense of the craters.

By this point in the war the 'Chain of Evacuation' of the wounded was well established. Men made their way – or were carried on stretchers – first to the Regimental Aid Post close to the front line, often in a dugout, where they were triaged and if possible, patched up and sent back to fight. The more severe cases were taken to a Field Ambulance Dressing Station, which was about half a mile or so behind the lines, often reached by tortuous and dangerous communication trenches. Here they might be given

---

[92] WSRO RSR MSS/7/11; Rutter [n.d.]: 60-65.

further treatment and sent back to their unit, or sent to the next stage, a Casualty Clearing Station about twelve miles behind the lines. This collection of tents had all the facilities to treat the very sick and severely wounded, with operating theatres and wards. Casualties were given urgent treatment and prepared for evacuation to a base hospital in France or Belgium by train or barge, and then, if necessary, by ship back to Blighty.

Ralph recalls visiting a Field Ambulance Dressing Station situated behind the lines in a cellar beneath a brewery in Vermelles. As well as giving an insight into the scene, he records a particularly poignant moment; amid the chaos a little dog gives a moment of comfort to a badly wounded man, tenderly licking his face. Ralph is clearly touched that the dog 'gives his sympathy with human intuition, the only one there who has time for such things'.[93]

According to the War Diary the battalion spent March and April moving in and out of the line in the Hohenzollern/Vermelles sector, spending only about three or four days in the front line due to the bad weather, snow and rain, the condition of the trenches and the frequent enemy action. In a letter to his mother dated March 28th, Ralph writes of this period, which he considered 'the worst I have experienced.'[94] While not in front line trenches they continued to undertake 'excessive' fatigues and many carrying parties, only having brief interludes when they were able to clean up and get some proper sleep.[95]

At the end of April they marched away from the war zone into rest. Ralph's appreciation of the burgeoning spring countryside is all the more ecstatic because of the contrast with the desolate landscape he had recently left. For the men as well as the countryside, there is a sense of rebirth and freedom from care as they laughed and gambolled like the boys many of them were. Ralph's celebration of the regenerative power of nature, something he returns to later in his memoir, is almost religious in its fervour. Here is a landscape artist using words to 'paint' the countryside and at the same time enjoying the parallels with his beloved Sussex Downs.[96]

Throughout May the battalion was at Lapugnoy enjoying an extended period of rest. Once again, the men were kept busy with training, inspections, parades, exercises at brigade and divisional level. Although there were suspicions about the reasons for all this activity, these were put to one side as they enjoyed what Ralph calls 'The Spring Holiday'.

[93] WSRO Add. Mss. 25005: 132, 135.
[94] See Appendix p. 269.
[95] WSRO RSR MSS/7/11.
[96] WSRO Add. Mss. 25005: 135-138.

But the holiday had to end and at the beginning of June 1916 the 7th Royal Sussex was a battalion in reserve. On 8th June they travelled by bus and foot to Bully Grenay and Maroc, small mining villages on the front line to the south of the Vermelles sector where they had previously been. After a few days working by night on fatigues and working parties and resting in the day, they moved to Douvrin, a village known as a jumping off point for a different part of the line. At this point rumours started to fly, with whispers of Egypt and Verdun as possible destinations: but it was a well kept secret and there was no mention of the actual destination. On 16th June the battalion travelled south by train and foot to Amiens, a journey vividly described by Ralph, then on to Vignacourt, where they stayed for the next two weeks, taking part in further intensive training and practice attacks with new drafts. On 28th June they moved to Fleselles.[97] From the sheer volume of men, guns, ammunition and supplies it was now obvious that something momentous was about to happen: they were all headed for the Somme.

Situated at the far south of the British section of the Western Front, the Somme region had seen little heavy fighting during the first two years of the war. The Germans occupied the most advantageous positions on high ground and had dug strong fortifications and deep trench systems in the well-drained, chalky ground. After a week-long, massive artillery barrage, on 1st July 1916 the British and Imperial forces attacked the Germans on an 18 mile front. It was the bloodiest day in the history of the British Army with almost 60,000 casualties of whom nearly 20,000 died. Few objectives were reached (except on the south of the sector where there was some success) and the battle was to continue for a further four and a half months until 18th November 1916.[98]

The 7th Royal Sussex were in reserve positions around Albert from the 1st to the 5th July, taking part in working parties and bomb-carrying, and they witnessed large numbers of wounded coming away from the line. On the 6th they went into trenches in preparation for an attack on Ovillers, which was still in German hands, on the 7th July.

The Battalion War Diary gives a detailed account of the attack on the 7th and 8th July: the fighting was fierce and despite coming under heavy fire and counter attack from the Germans, by noon they had reached their first and second objectives, but abandoned their third objectives, as the C.O. decided instead to consolidate the new positions. Around noon it started to rain, and continued throughout the day, 'making the trenches into a kind of porridge mud'. During the night of the 7th fresh supplies of ammunition and water were brought up and they continued to consolidate and defend the new positions on the 8th July, until they were relieved that night. Casualties (killed,

---

[97] WSRO RSR MSS/7/11.
[98] For further information refer to: Sheffield (2003); Middlebrook (2016).

wounded and missing) during the two days were 21 out of 25 officers and 440 out of 650 other ranks.[99]

But where was Ralph? In Volume IV he writes only that on the 6th July he was at Henencourt, where he heard the 'pounding of the guns', knowing that his comrades were in the front line waiting to go over the top, and from where he watched the depleted battalion return after the attack on the 8th July. In the 1948 revised edition he reveals that before the attack he received orders to report to Divisional Head Quarters at Henencourt and he 'went no further with the battalion. My fate whenever the 7th went into action'. He does not elucidate further. With such heavy casualties, it is possible this saved his life, but Ralph clearly felt guilty about being a 'fair weather soldier'.[100]

Moving back for a much needed clean up and rest, on the 12th July the battalion received a visit from General Scott, commander of 12th Division, to congratulate them on the capture of Ovillers. With the battalion at under half strength, new drafts came in, but both the War Diary and Ralph's account bemoan the fact that they were of a poor standard, with the Medical Officer finding about fifty per cent unfit.[101] For Ralph, the loss of so many of the men with whom he had served from the outset, and the introduction of drafts, often from different localities without the sense of attachment to Sussex, changed the character of the battalion. To add to the confusion many of the drafts were sent to the wrong units, a situation that was quickly rectified. On the 25th July the commanding officer of the battalion, Lt. Col. Osborn left to take over the command of the 16th Infantry Brigade; the men were sad to see him go. Lt. Col Alfred Sansom succeeded him.

On 27th July the 7th Royal Sussex was in the support line at the Ovillers/La Boiselle line, supplying the front line trenches with bombs and water. These trenches had been part of the German front line system before the 1st July: the comfort and spaciousness of the deep German dug-outs were a source of fascination, as was the detritus left by their former inhabitants, although in the heat the stench of death was overwhelming. Passing over the land that had been so bitterly fought for and that had claimed so many casualties, especially from Ralph's own battalion, was an upsetting experience. From the 30th July to 4th August, the battalion occupied front line trenches west of Pozieres (which was captured by the Australians earlier in the month) taking part in a series of attacks, with varying success, and sustaining 10 officer casualties and 214 other ranks. Volume IV finishes at this point, at the end of the 7th Royal Sussex's second tour of duty in the Somme battle.

---

[99] WSRO RSR MSS/7/11; see also Rutter [n.d.]: 84-93.
[100] WSRO Add. Mss. 25001: 102; for a personal account of the fighting at Ovillers see the memoir of Charles Tulett, WSRO, RSR Museum Acc. 3179.
[101] WSRO RSR MSS/7/11: 16-17 July 1916; WSRO Add. Mss. 25005: 156, 159.

In the fourth volume Ralph's images are mostly of landscapes and buildings he observed when behind the lines. They act as illustrations for his account, which in the second half of this volume follows the chronology of the movements of the 7th Royal Sussex more closely. With a few sketches of his comrades and local inhabitants, the focus is on the French countryside; both untouched and scarred by the war. Views from observation posts give an impression of what Ralph saw when he looked out into no man's land, an unusual perspective for an infantryman, and contrast with the relative normality behind the lines. During the 'Spring Holiday' at Lapugnoy he obviously had more time for drawing and painting and produced a few bright water colours, which contrast with the monochrome tones of the images closer to the front. However, in this volume it is the narrative that brings the experiences of an infantryman on the Western Front into sharp relief.

Sketch from O.Pip. Border Redoubt: shewing four lines of German trenches and Douvrin Distillery.

. . Fosse 8 . .

Bombing Posts.

From north to south the opposing lines swung near to and far from each other, from thirty yards to hundreds of yards apart, the Hun invariably having at that time the choice of ground; and from north to south one might think that trenches were the same, in a general way of course they were. To those who came there, the same purpose existed, to defend and to kill, also there was the same remoteness from the pre-war life, which includes all the days spent away from the active zone of war.

But every little sector of line seemed to possess its own individuality, its own method of carrying on the war and these methods were handed over to each successive relief, as part of that particular trenches property.

There were parts of the line, that demanded, a free use of the rifle, but in the next sector of line to be occupied, the rifle would almost be forgotten and the rifle grenade would be the chosen weapon of offense. In the Vermelles sector, it was the bombers, who carried on the offensive spirit.

A bit of line, one or two hundred yards long, possessing its watchful sentries, remained quiet, the rifle seldom used, except at night, when a sentry would fire now and then, more to amuse and to keep himself awake, than for any other purpose, firing at the spot where a very light had suddenly shot upwards from; or, answering the spurt of vivid light from the Hun sentries rifle; the bullets seldom finding a human billet, but more often, whistling too high over the trench, to drop a thousand yards or more in rear, harmlessly in open deserted places, or tapping at the broken tiles, flattening against the brickwork of the ruined houses of the little village in rear.

But dividing up the line, were the bombing posts, ugly, narrow and snake like were the short trenches, saps we called them; that ran out from the main trench, to get within throwing distance of the Hun, and there the war was carried on.

Some bombers were keen and active, delighting in throwing bombs, but more often the bombs dropped and burst just without their mark, so that the soil about was very dark, torn and ploughed continually.

There was one bombing pit, a little uglier than the many. The narrow trench, dug through the soft, squidgy mud, curved and twisted, then left you in a big shell hole, cleaned out a very little, so that three or four men could move about there, a steel loop-hole was fixed to the further side and one man watched, and gave warning when the Hun hand grenade, swiftly appeared above the top of the mud bank thirty to fourty yards away; a weighted stick with streamers flying to steady its flight. After the burst, the other two, good throwers both, answered with three bombs to every one they sent.

Here they lived, for many hours at a time; pressing and crouching against the further mud bank, when the bombs burst. Sitting on the full and empty bomb boxes, their furniture; half buried in the soft soil, eating their food with hands dirty from touching everything polluted with mud, unclean mud too, men have been buried here and the bursting bombs, disturbs the soil that covers them, the rain too releases and beats down the parapit; and on one side it reveals, its feet still held by the mud, a shrunken rotting body, hanging downwards, a ghastly ridicule of the physique of a man, his hair seems to have grown and hangs straight down, long, dank and sodden, as though it would part company from the head.

On the left, the bank of the trench is but three feet high, then widens out to the further side of the shell hole; the intervening space is a mass of mud with fragments of rusty, vicious looking barbed wire jutting from it, and looking closely, for the mud

. . The main road between Noyelles and Mazingarbe. . .

Sketch from an Artillery. O.Pip. shewing British & German trenches, the 2 black dots are old german light railway trucks and serve to denote No-mans-land. British trenches to the right of these. Douvrin Church & Distillery on the ridge.

has dyed everything with its ugly uniform colouring; one sees the portions of other bodies uncovered, a round head, an arm, the elbow thrust up like a capital A without the cross bar.

One is glad to get away from here, it is too much like dwelling in a charnel-house, and these thudding, bursting bombs make such a condition, a very near and personal possibility to all who come there in great health and strength. The bombers seem not to notice it, taking great interest in the flight of their bombs and in giving plenty of interest for all they receive.

They have observed one lively Hun bomber, a cheeky impudent youngster, unlike the many, who will sometimes look up, after they have thrown, with laughter and ridicule in his face: Their best throwing efforts fail to quench his irritating humour of the game, so they send a pressing message to a chum, a sniper, and he arrives in hot haste, like a hunter hearing where rare, good game may be bagged; They throw again and he watches for the boyish, jeering face, then seeing, seeks carefully and cunningly for a place along the little narrow trench, where he may raise his head and rifle, so slowly, amidst the hummocks of mud, and see — steadily — resting just above the tip of the sights — the spot, where the foolish and over-bold will raise his head.

Again our bomber throws, purposely short this time.

A little patient waiting and for the last time the target appears. The sniper aimed truly and is as full of glee for the remainder of the day, as the hunter, who brings down his first rare game.

Nœux les Mines from Noyelles – Sailly Labourse road.

. . A Hun Attack. . .

One feature of this sector was the continuous uncertainty of action to be expected from the enemy. The Hun evidently had this feeling about ourselves too, not only when mining took the most active form of offense, but before that time and he shewed his uneasiness with sudden bursts of shelling that played havoc with our support and reserve trenches: and at night with feverish displays of coloured very lights, that told of men anxious for the reassuring support of their artillery before ever it was needed.

It was just after "stand down" at evening, we occupied Northampton trench, a support line 70 yards in rear of the front line. A Battalion of the Middlesex Regiment was on our left.

There was just a warm glow of light left in the sky above the dark earth, silent and cold that ran up to meet and contrasted so strongly against it. Then quite without warning a section of line, away to the right and almost on to the skyline became enveloped in smoke and this volume of smoke was the birthplace of sudden, clustering, rapier blades of flame that illuminate the smoke, the earth around with a bloody glow; are gone; yet are continuous, so swiftly another takes its place, burst after burst, up and down that short bit of line.

Every man is turned out and takes his place on the fire step, the S.A.A and bombs are looked to, to see that they are immediately available.

Fragments of shell, hiss and scream away over head, or come to earth near with a forceful thud, but the shelling is not for us. At this comparitively safe distance those bursting "crumps", fascinate and excite; and the sensation of sight is much more absorbing than the sensation of hearing; the scream of the approaching shells may be heard and the tearing, blasting burst of noise forms a background for all, but one watches with fascinated interest for the red upward shooting, tongues of flame.

There is a genuine hope with most that the Hun will attack and a keen readiness to handle rifle and bomb to the best of our ability. But he attacks, only where he has hoped to crush out of existence any form of resistance and as one watches that belt of surging smoke and volcanic eruptions, one wonders if any man can possibly have lived through it.

The belt of broken and scared earth that unites our trench with the german position on the higher ground, lies black against the faint light remaining in the sky. The gun-fire lessens; nothing may be seen in that deep velvet blackness of earth, but as objects rise above the skyline, so they become visible like moving silhouettes, looking larger, yet vague in outline, than their normal size. Soon after the gun-fire commenced, an object rose up, black and huge against the red glow of flame on smoke; it caught the eye and the imagination for a moment, so strange it seemed, spreading large wings and big head thrust forward, flying heavily towards us, low over the earth, like a great symbol of evil and death. It was but an owl.

And now our machine guns are rattling away in fury, figures are seen running and scrambling forward over parapit and crumpled soil, to take up forward positions and drive out the few Huns who have managed to invade a few of our forward saps and the smashed front line that will need so much repairing after the rough handling it has received this night.

One other attack of another kind we just escaped. We had been relieved by the

. . Noyelles . .

15th Scottish Division. The relief came by day, and the day was bright and clear. The Hun from his observation balloons, may have seen the platoons of men, one after the other at short intervals between each — come up the road from Annequin into Vermelles, or it may have been just luck that made him choose a day when a relief was in progress to send his clouds of gas and smoke across to our lines.

Our Battalion had just arrived in billets at Annequin, and we were taking our first meal, sitting in the bare houses or in the unkempt gardens surrounding them, for Annequin was a mining village and had been planed more or less on modern lines. So the alarm came, but before that, we had seen what appeared to be, a wall of mist approaching, as a thick mist will come up out of the sea, so quietly as appearing not to move, yet came swiftly and its first clinging, poisonous folds, that blotted out the high light and radiance of the day, was with us almost before our smoke helmets were adjusted.

At this distance behind the lines, its effects may not have proved fatal without a helmet, but the animals, the only helmetless ones — for the civilians dwelling there possessed them — found it troublesome, and the horses and mules were taken out and sent galloping before it across the waste ground towards Bethune, where even there its effects were felt. One or two dogs of the village succombed to the attack.

This area affected parts of two divisions occupying the line, one, very well disciplined and practised in the rapid adjusting of respirators, suffered but few casualties, the other who had less fully appreciated the value and enforced the irritating methods and discipline of gas helmet drill suffered in consequence. The Hun was wily too, using gas, then smoke, gas again and so on in varying

Sketch from an Artillery O. Pip, shewing Fosse 8, La Bassee in distance and the tangle of British & German trenches.

Times, so that the men knew not what to expect, and thinking, when the smoke arrived, that the gas was finished, threw aside their helmets. To be caught fatally by the next wave of gas.

.. Wiring ..

Fixing up wire defences, is a task that varies considerably with the nature of the ground, the nearness and activity of the Hun. There were parts of the line where the wire was broad and strong, because it was possible to take out large wiring parties and so keep it in good repair or add to it as much as was required. Then wiring became but a nuisance, that kept one from sleep during half the night; but where the two opposing lines were close or on an active part of the line, then this night work might be far from unexciting.

At the Hohenzollern redoubt, the two lines crested this slight wave of ground, which made it difficult, even at night, for men to move about in no-mans-land unseen. But there was one advantage, the ground was a series of shell holes, and when a Machine gun spat out its sudden hate, there was always a convenient cavity at hand to drop into.

Now the ground here had been fought over, and many had been the casualties, left out there, buried and unburied, it was all the same when the shells came, tore up the earth, as though with huge clawing hands, the bodies too, splintered

Vermelles.

stakes and the wire, churned it all up; then the rains beat down upon it and sank deeply into the loose mass.

Many things are easily forgotten, because they are often repeated, only those made more striking by rather unusual conditions, stand out clearly in the memory to form the nucleus of that particular kind of experience. In thinking of wiring parties, ones mind naturally recalls this particular sector, when with at most two men to help, — for men were scarce, for other work than sentry duty, — creeping out over the parapit into that soft, squidgy, evil mess; when the sky had wrapped itself in a mantle of deep blackness and the atmosphere was laden with a fine, soaking rain. Then setting about uncoiling a reel or two of barbed wire, in and out amongst the old strands of wire and stakes, up and down those hummocks and deep holes. None can quite picture the nature of such ground and the experience of crawling and scrambling in and out from one shell hole to another, unwinding the wire, being caught and held by the barbs on old strands, The thick, wet clayey soil clinging to hands and clothes, the very light that for a moment or two makes one remain motionless, with face turned away from the light — to see — at ones feet, the portion of a body, turned up in tortured pose with the battered soil. There seems to be a portion of a body in almost every shell hole, and as one moves backwards and forwards, making the entanglement thicker, sliding down into these cavities, one begins to recognise them by these repulsive figures. They have done their work, and greatly, but one cannot help speaking of them as being such, on suddenly finding oneself bending low over a misshapen, evil smelling form, they possess this dark, sodden soil, limbs, grotesque and vague meet you

Vermelles Church.

frequently, sticking out from the soft earth, and one is glad to work hard, get out the required amount of wire and return to the comparitively clean trench, the company of living men, tired, with every tissue in the body used up and crying for rest and sleep.

·· Crater fighting at the Hohenzollern Redoubt. ··

It was during the first few days of March 1916, that the stiffest work was undertaken in this sector. About that time my leave came along, arriving back in the line after all the work for our Battalion was finished.

After months of strenuous sapping, galleries had been dug at a great depth, right beneath the German front lines. Three mines were sprung at once, all near to each other, flinging those Huns occupying the deep dug outs and those forward positions, in a flash, to — wherever they were bound for.

Men of the Royal Fusiliers then went forward to occupy the craters, and the task fell to our Battalion to relieve these men after the craters were taken and hold on to them.

Returning from leave and being dumped at Bethune, in the small hours of a cold morning, with snow falling, made for the Divisional Stores, there to spend the remainder of the night; here for the first time, heard rumours of what the

THE CRATER ZONE.

Looking on to the Hohenzollern Redoubt from Alexandra Trench.

The Church. Lapugnoy.

Brigade was doing. In the morning, packed up and marched on to Sailly-Labourse where our Transport lay; and the faces of the men here were longer, so too their tales of woe [they love to encourage men going up to the line], but there was no disputing the fact of the large number of casualties lying in the School, — used too as a Divisional Canteen, waiting for ambulances to take them further back.

That night we moved up with the ration limbers to Vermelles, and eventually arrived in the line and saw the huge craters and how it was our casualties were so many. After this experience, craters were held from the near outer lip and not from the forward inner lip, — to make a target for every kind of projectile the enemy may care to pump into it, as he did there. The largest of these craters was from 60 to 70 feet across and almost as deep. In face of the terrific pounding they received and the counter-attacks by bomb made upon them, the men held on, one or two bombing without rest almost, certainly without sleep for 24 hours at a stretch. The task of bringing up those bombs, was as great, the weather could not have been worse, heavy snow fell, that melted into the soil and with the constant shelling, that tore down the walls of the trenches, making a mass of thick, heavy mud almost impossible to drag ones feet through. Here, the casualties were many too, in walking round, it was easy to see, how great and unpleasant an experience one had missed. Here and there in the support line, the dead occupied the fire step, or had been hastily thrust into broken parapit and partly built over with sand-bags, in the little short saps. They lay crumpled and bent, out of the way of the living, struggling up and down the heavily mud clogged trench, with sand-bags filled with bombs, so that orders might be carried out, — to hold on.

In the big crater, the sun shone and the men were cheerier than any one had met in the safer places at Sailly or Bethune. The relief was coming that day, some rations and cigarettes too had at last arrived ; and a skylark had risen from somewhere out of that stark, shell ploughed ground, where the still dead lay and winged its way upwards into the clear, clean atmosphere, singing a promise of new life, greater than we knew of, so why should they think of those forms, both Hun and English, lying together, hacked and twisted in the hollow of the crater.

But what of the wounded ? In such a place and under such conditions how did they fare ? The Field Ambulance Dressing Station was situated in the big cellar beneath the remains of the brewery at Vermelles, — a long way from the line when measured by those shell searched, tortuous communication trenches.— The brick steps leading from the concrete floor, where, over head the remaining girders and framework of roof, so twisted, formed grotesque patterns against the sky ; led down into the low roofed cellar, where the eyes were at once attracted by the brightly, candle lit tables at the further end and the white robed doctors moving busily about them. Then the eye took in the larger scene and saw in the dimness, the figures of men on stretchers, resting on the brick floor, others less badly damaged sit close up by the side wall, all are covered with the mud, an orderly is carefully cutting away the mud clotted clothing of one resting on a rough table, near by the lighted candles.

But there is one incident that suddenly becomes the central group of this scene, arresting the eye, it is so full of poignancy and rare humanity, all else fades

. . The Crucifix Lapugnoy. . .

Road from Lapugnoy to Allouagne.

away into the background. There on the brick floor, lies a figure, but just where he is hit, none could say at a glance, so plastered is he with mud from head to foot, he has fallen face downwards into it, and of his face, as he lies there, only his fine white teeth are noticeable, with the lips slightly drawn back, the remainder of the face is a smear of mud, but no noise escapes those tightly clenched teeth; and there, — not a yard away, is a little mongrel dog, and he is straining, straining his body forward, until without moving his stiffened legs, with tongue outstretched, - he, — just manages, to quietly lick the mud covered face. There is so little to distinguish that quiet, prone figure from the earth, but that bit of a dog seems to know by instinct, that here lies a man friend, suffering, and gives of his sympathy with human intuition and tenderness, the only one there who has time for such things.

. . The Spring Holiday. . .

Spring had arrived again, the skylarks were the first to tell us, as they rose up from the untrodden ground and one marvelled at there choice, those fields where the dead still lay. Sometimes a pair of magpies, in their bold colouring and undulating flight, crossed from one territory to another, seeking and not finding, old and favoured spots for the new years living and a few spring flowers grew up out of the little gardens, choked with the rubbish from the shattered houses.

But <u>spring</u> is a radiant glory, made up of thousands of mating birds, thousands

. . Near Allouagne. . .

of flowers, a pulsating host of minute things, gently but surely being brought into life; and they come throbbing through the air, up out of the earth, a hundred thousand voices, clothed in wonderful garments of every shape and colour, so, you may hear them if you listen, — chanting, praising the God who gave them life.

It was just when these things were happening, that we left the line for a long spell in rest. Marching back, away from the Winter of desolation, where the spring of new life, could only just trickle through, in such few ways.

The romance and joy of the winding road came to us again, in greater force than ever, every bend, revealed a vision of the earth, undevastated, less foul and greener; until we came to a halt, remembered; because of the little wood, there by the roadside. I think it was here that we ate our lunch. But the wood whilst it throbbed with activity, arraying itself, with oxlips and anemones peeping out from its raiment of changing greens, partly thrown over the old dress of browns; told us clearly, how the world was and how far spring had advanced. Winter had been with us till then.

I think when we took to the road again, that the drummers ahead, played more lustily, the men caught the spirit and life of the day, swung along the road without a care in the world, singing words to the lively airs played by the fifes, bringing the people dwelling in the wayside houses and villages, the women workers in the fields, running to the roadside, to watch these joyful marching men pass by.

We marched on by the bye ways, until we came again to the main road, with its border of tall trees, their high branches, faintly tinged with green, the spreading fields to right and left, bearing a new verdure of fruitful growth, the earth sang, it was a great world to be in; and so we came to Lillers and rested again beyond, on a spur of high ground that was dressed in a gay little frock, the fashion of our Sussex Downs, of fine grasses and little flowers; and untired men,—boys, pack free, unable to rest awhile quietly, gamboled, throwing clods of clean earth and grass at each other and laughed again.

On to the road once more, through country that had never known war and finally to our destination at Lapugnoy.

At Lapugnoy we grew sleek and fit, of course sometimes the question, must steal into the mind. For what reason are we so treated, trained and fitted? But the lottery of war holds many chances, men let the thought of death, labour in their minds, and death claims them for his own. He would have been a fool to allow thoughts of such harsh, crude things, filter into his mind, when all the earth about was rejoicing, and those woods, so beautiful, breeding a wealth of our English woodland flowers and a little later, a multitude of Lily-'o-the-valley, half hid amongst crowding green verdure. Here one might sit in the early morning, after tumbling into the almost ice cold, swiftly running stream and listen to the great hum of all the little things, the noisy clatter of the jays and the placid satisfied cooing of the pigeons, with the sunlight glittering through the trees.

There was a large Casualty Clearing Station here, near to the road, but the British Cemetery,— accompaniment to every C.C.S.— lay tucked away on the slope of a hill, and a motherly wood, stretched her shielding branches almost about it, then pleasant pasture land, caressed it and pointed to a glimpse of the blue haunting lands in the distance.

Each Sunday, when the weather was fine, came the womenfolk and children, up out of the village, walked through the woods, gathering as they went, bunches of wild

British Cemetery at 18th C.C.S. Lapugnoy.

flowers, bluebells, lily o' the valley and laid them, a bunch for each at the foot of the little crosses, bearing the name of the man, his regiment and those poignant words, — Died of Wounds.

We remained at Lapugnoy until June, 1916, carrying out the usual training. The Division was then moved, and our Brigade made a days march to Estree Blanche, where we were billeted in the remains of a large Factory which had been partly destroyed by a boiler explosion.

During a rest, the training usually takes the same course, in a more or less condensed form, beginning with very elementary squad drill etc and finishing if possible with training that will give Brigades and Divisional staffs a little exercise in handling their men in the field and for all the various units to work together in unison. Naturally it is often difficult to obtain the ground for these larger exercises, it may have been for that reason we moved here, the country was open enough and undulating, but everywhere cultivated, however a large area had been marked off for the use of the Brigade, and we began our training in open attack, through the patches of wheat, oats, roots &etc with which the ground was divided up, in small strips and patches.

About two days were so occupied, then came the order to move quite suddenly and in an hour we had packed up, were on the road once more, marching back to Lapugnoy.

One would liked to have seen more of that village, or some parts of it that stretched along the little valley, one or two quaint old houses were there, and two interesting chateaus, one in particular, aged, complete with wide moat and drawbridge, set

· · Willows by the stream, Lapugnoy. · ·

The Mill, Estree Blanche.

amongst shaded by great elms and a few firs, lush meadows watered by clear running streams, bordered by lovely willows, bending down as though entranced with their own beauty reflected in the clear stream. This village had known other troops, more gaily arrayed than we and the stone walls of the Church bore the splintered marks of Prussian bullets, souvenirs of the Franco Prussian War.

The return to Lapugnoy marked the close of this summer holiday, for so it seemed and serious work loomed up largely ahead. It came first with fatigue parties being called for to dig cable trenches up there about the old ground near Vermelles, the men being carried off dressed in fighting order with the addition of a pick or spade to carry, in the afternoon by a number of old motor omnibuses, returning in the small hours of the morning by the same means. In a day or two these same 'buses carried us all away. We were a division in reserve and might be sent here or there, wherever it might be greatly needed along our front. Until then we had been fortunate, resting and training peacefully, but now work had been found for us, and so we were whisked away back to war. The 'buses carrying us almost into Grenay, which left us to march but a short way into Bully Grenay. Here part of the battalion was billeted, the remainder marched on up the hill and found shelter in Moroc.

These mining villages were just a little further south of the Vermelles sector, a deep railway cutting divided this high ground on which Moroc was built, whilst the other villages sprawled out over the land, running one into the other, a landscape painted with the blue-grey of slate roof and red brick, made more striking in places by the quaint dark pyramidical forms of the slag heaps, around which the houses clustered more closely. Amongst all those buildings, how many

. . Corner of Chateau . Estree Blanche . . .

remain whole, undamaged? A few were smashed utterly, and few, too, were altogether unspoilt, and this had been a village of distinction, possessing houses well built and set about with gardens, where now soldiers, with an eye for form and colour, and a pride of regiment, had laid out with great skill and ingenuity, a mosaic work formed of bits of tile, slate, chalk and coloured glass, a decorative representation of their regimental crest. The houses on the further slope of the ridge, came within view of the German lines, so many were smashed, and all were deserted. The school was here, and had once formed a strong point, desk and forms were piled high, reinforced with sandbags to form a barrier, but shells had searched it, pierced its walls, brought portions of the roof crashing in, and made a chaos of it all, untenable. The gardens still bore a picking of fruit and vegetables, for those who cared to seek, with one eye for these things and the other on the visibility of their person.

Our nights here were spent in digging a new trench out somewhere in the open, on the far side of the big mine and its circle of work-sheds, that by night and day drew the fire of the Hun gunners. A little whiff of blue smoke or steam? — told him of a shaft that was being kept clear, so he sent high explosives, bursting about it, trying to utterly destroy it. The adjoining yard containing a large store of pit props of all lengths, were useful for rivetting trenches, and those shells that visited so near at such irregular hours, made the fatigue parties detailed for the gathering of the pit props very nimble and quick about the job.

    By day we slept, ate, wrote our letters, and met occasionally old friends, who had left us long since, wounded, to be returned to the 2nd battalion who were then holding the line before Moroc.

    Again we moved, marching back through a succession of mining villages, to Douvrin.

· Chateau · Flesselles ·

This village was remembered as the jumping off place for quite a different part of the line, also for the number of rumours that grew up like mushrooms in a night, as to our des--tination, for it was known our stay here would be short, and the rumours ranged from Verdun to Egypt, in either case a warm spot, and in this the rumours were correct. Now when rumours spring up in such great strength, one may be sure that they have been set afoot with a purpose, and they have their uses. It was whilst toiling a great distance up to a bad part of the line, intensely fatigued, that the little voice of rumour came, gaily tripping from man to man, whispering to each that the Dardanelles had been forced. It did not lighten our load, or make the way shorter, but gave us something cheerful to think about, someone was winning, and the man who set that untruth sailing up the of men, must have been inspired, so to do.

Now we were going somewhere, and a place must be named, so an important looking officer splashed with red, whispers Verdun to a battalion commander, with whom he dines. Another acts in a similar way over a whiskey and soda, but in a voice just loud enough for the waiting mess orderly to hear, speaks of Egypt. So they go speeding from mouth to mouth, and the word Somme rests peacefully, unthought of.

Entraining, added to the delusion of travelling a great distance, not that we cared much where we were taken. These were new scenes we were passing through, clean beautiful country, to be enjoyed in the seeing, and the speed of the train gave us plenty of time to admire it. Sometimes, hustling along with sudden haste, as though remembering that it had set out to reach a certain place, then slowing down, stopping altogether, as a child that hurries along the road, then lingers, and is stayed by the prettiness of wayside flowers, so we made a wide circle of a journey, which we imagined might be taking us far south, and the nature of the country changed, a tideless river intersect--ing lush green meadows, could be seen through the interstices of the branches of trees, planted in straight rows and cut to to a general uniform pattern, but very tall and beautiful they looked in that luxurious green land, that nearer to Amiens was devoted to the growth of much fruit and vegetables, well watered by the little dykes that cut it up into a small squared pattern of intensive cultivation.

We passed through Amiens to a little wayside station, more fitted for the detraining of troops and guns; arriving early in the evening were formed up almost immediately and marched, much to our surprise and pleasure, back through the city, which had seen Prussian soldiers too march through its wide streets. Many people watched the brigade march through, an unusual experience for us, and we made the most of it, trying to create an impression, swinging along like veterans in perfect condition, with drum and fife sounding their best.

We did not halt until the outskirts of the city were reached, just as day was departing and the fine, needle-like spire of the Cathedral, and all the buildings are etched blackly against a background of red, shading to orange; day, flaunting its last glorious light, that blended into the neutral twilight colours, green to purplish blue, and there met the great curtain of clouded night that had come up out of the East, sending out advance tongues of cloud touched with the flame colour of the departed sun.

Day departed with the life and movement of those city streets, and the quiet night marched with us, when we again took to the road, a never ending road it seemed, through country unpopulated, for the night was dark, shutting out all that lay beyond the border of the road.

In the early hours of the morning we arrived at Vignacourt, very weary, for a twelve to fifteen miles march in full marching order, coming on top of a tiring day's railway journey, cramped up in cattle trucks, is not an easy way of spending the greater part of 24 hours.

Bivouacs, in reserve, [Long Valley].

We thought the march had brought us nearer to the line again, and it was with some suprise that we learnt the following morning that the front was many miles from here. It was as though a new lease of life had been given to us, to find that instead of being into the line again, we were to stay for a couple of weeks in this big straggling, farming community, almost all the houses appeared to be a farm on a small scale, two or three cows are kept, a horse, or a pony, and many fowls. Agricultural land, plotted out in many shapes and shades of colour, stretched away up and down the waves of ground, as far as the eye could see, with here and there a densely grown wood, villages few and far between. The wonder was that the remaining inhabitants of these farming centres, elderly men and women, could cope with the amount of work to be dealt with on these big stretches of farm land.

Rumours now began to take more definite shape. There was a lot of talk of big things happening for which we knew we were now to rehearse; to some the thought of it came like the expectancy of going a great journey, when many new sights and new sensations would be the daily experience, and to others it was like looking into a deep pit, out of which there was little hope of escaping. Darkness and the terror of darkness, dwelt there. But to the great majority who had become enured to this life of movement, marching, working, watching and fighting, at all hours of the day and night, taking sleep, rest and pleasure whenever it might come their way, to these the future could look after itself. Fate was their God, and decided whether they must live or die. So it was no use bothering about what was before. A sound religion for a fighting soldier, perhaps.

Bus-les-Artois.

The spirit of men dwelling together is sometimes lifted and held by one man,[who may be a private or N.C.O], just as the reverse effect may be the case. The Commanding Officer by his very position must influence the whole battalion in some way or other. We were fortunate to be commanded by a man who did demand a high level of discipline, combined with an understanding fairness and regard for the men under his command, which drew forth the best qualities in all ranks. But in a section or platoon one strong character often greatly influences the spirit of the other men, and one remembers one man here in particular, who had always shown a great disregard of fear, a boisterous humour, and a keen desire to fight. The future was almost rosy to him and held no fear, and he expressed his attitude towards the immediate future whenever he came to rest, almost the last, in the little barn, divided into three departments by wood partitions. He treated his partition as a parapet, dashed at it, scrambling over, shouting out the catch phrase of that time, "Over the top with the best of luck". It was no use for those unfortunate men peacefully lying wrapt in great coat on whom he came tumbling and yelling, to complain. Cheeseman's humour and elan had to be borne with cheer-
-fully, but the Somme battlefield finally claimed him.
There was one Sergeant who, too, had little fear and a great ambition, and hoped to win the most coveted of decorations, and he went forward to claim this as his prize, but Fate dealt with him less kindly, striking him brutally in the face with flying metal on the first day of battle.
So men go forward together, but remote from each other in spirit and aim.

The big sham attacks were done with, and we marched away with a feeling that

La-Boisselle

we were leaving the summer behind, with the peace and quietness and that wide expanse of open country. Flesselles was our first halting place, and we were like a little stream that here joined the main river, pressing forward on its surface, a continuous stream of troops, all night the artillery rumbled past and cavalry too, though little they were needed. But it filled us with high hopes and great expectancy. The battalions were as fit as ever they had been; the new drafts recently joined had been given time to feel a responsible part of their Unit, and all were in first rate health and condition.

We continued the march by dusty roads that had never before borne such a host of marching men, guns and transport, past village and hamlet, choc-a-bloc with troops, halting for a night in village which other troops had but just evacuated, to take part in the first day's battle.

We met some returning, crowded into G.S. waggons, or any spare vehicle, the bandage on head or limb showing clean and white against the soiled clothing, the slightly wounded, smiling, happy and optimistic.

The traffic of the road had changed, it had borne forward a nation's pride of men in all their fine physique; now, enveloped in dust that rises in dense clouds from the constant stream of infantry, guns, lorries, and every vehicle of war, one after the other, swift, quiet running, motor ambulances, carried back these men, the greatest wastage that war begets.

From Henencourt one listened all through the night of July 6th to the pounding of the guns, knowing that one's own battalion was up there in the midst of it all, waiting sleeplessly for the moment to go over, and dawn brought a sight of German shrapnel, quantities of it, continuously bursting on the high ground beyond Aveluy, but Ovillers was ours.

· Albert ·

Airman may bring back to headquarters exact information of the enemy lines, the disposition of their forces and harrass them with bomb or machine gun, the gunners hammer their defences to nought, but it is the infantry that must weather the storm of flying metal and grasp the prize, hold on to it, though he in his turn may be pounded back into the soil, and when their strength grows weak others come to take their place, and the remnants of the original force return.

From the high wall about the big chateau of Henencourt we watched them march back, the glad reaction that comes from deliverance out of such a hell was in their bearing, and pride too in having done all that was expected of them.

A summer spent in training, fitting for the arena, now, after so few days, how short a stretch of road each battalion needs, the Companies are but platoons at full strength. Yet these are the chief actors in this great drama, no military status founded in days of peace can rob them of that pride of place. The fact is borne in on everyone, who watches these small battalions marching back, hugging the right of the road, to give room and to spare for the more imposing units streaming backwards and forwards, but which, afterall, are auxillary to the great Infantry the fighting unit.

After Ovillers the Brigade rested and recuperated in the woods at Bus-les-Artois, woods that had lost their freshness, owing to the number of troops which had passed through them, but the smart plumaged, chattering magpies were there, the sun in the foliage above, and the quiet and peace that every forest of trees imposes on all. At first our numbers gave us plenty of elbow room in the semicircular huts, but new men arrived to be initiated into the ways and character of the battalion.

· Bouzincourt ·

Corner of Front line trench, Agny.

Drafts were being sent to battalions in great haste, and without much thought, so that we received batches of Royal Fusiliers and Middlesex men, whilst they received men from our Regiment, much to everyone's annoyance. But this was quickly readjusted by a mutual arrangement between battalions. Men are seldom pleased to wear another regimental badge, and work better with their own units.

In these days drafts arrived frequently and disappeared as quickly, sometimes bringing with them one or two men of the original battalion, and always taking a few away. The roll of a platoon changed continually; the new men were not always up to the standard set in the earlier days, and with each draft there were one or two that the medical officer would refuse to accept, unfit for the job, men plucked from a useful civilian occupation, passed fit for general service by men who had no idea of what was demanded of an infantryman, is trained and fitted whatever the expense per man may be, arrives finally with his appointed unit, useless, drifts back down the line, to be absorbed into that large host the menial servants of an army.

Our commanding Officer left us here, and he will not easily forget the send-off that he was given, every man crowded to the steep wooded slope that bordered the road, none too many who knew him well, but we impressed the new men with a sense of our regard for him, so they came too and helped to swell the roar of cheers that echoed beneath the arch of trees. The car and the white road bore him away to the Brigade he was to command, our highest esteem and goodwill going with him.

Dainville Church.

La Boiselle & Pozieres.

The days were hot with a summer's heat, the roads again thick with dust that rose in clouds when our feet trod their surface once more towards the great arena, for a deep depth from the actual fighting area the country accommodates a vast concourse, not onlookers that crowded and surrounded those old small places of contest, but the combatants themselves, moving in and out of the fight, and like the combatants of old they stripped free for the encounter, leaving all they do not need in this thickly populated belt of country; so you may see encamped in the fields and orchards about the villages, the transport of the infantry, horse lines of the gunners, engineers, stores of every description, and sometimes cavalry, waiting for their chance.

The infantry and their transport are the most restless of this constantly moving army. They fill the villages, over-run into the fields around, as we did in moving up into action again.

It was the best that the billeting party could find for us, every barn in the village was full of troops, as we could easily see in marching through. Soldiers like to watch other troops pass by, and criticise them, in a detached sort of way, so they stood at the wide open doors of the big poorly built barns and houses that, without waste of ground, closely bordered the road. We passed on, just beyond the village, then wheeled to the left into the field shut off from the road by a high hedge. There was just enough room for our own, and the Middlesex Battalion to pile arms in close parallel lines. For the two nights spent here we lay down between the rows of equipment and stacked rifles, with great coat flung over,

Gas alarm bell at Agny.

watched the last of the day fade away, and the great expanse of sky above become like soft dark velvet, set with a thousand gems, listen to the joke and laughter of the men around, feel the cool night air caress the face and sleep whilst we may.

Through Aveluy our road lay, then dipped down to the little flooded valley, where men bathed and sometimes shells, lifting the water high into the air like a water-spout. Up on to the next ridge, past a succession of our disused trenches, then down again, across the old No Man's Land. We are marching across ground that but a few days ago was bolted and barred against us. To those who are called upon to pay the price, it seems a rather heavy one. This ground is ours, and the men who paid for it rest there, and they are many. A little further to the left is Ovillers and soil that covers many men who not long ago marched with us. We feel like baring our heads, doing something to express our feeling for comrades who have given their all that we may march on.

It gives us great satisfaction to explore the past strength and apparent security and comfort of this German position at La Boiselle. Its dug-outs started from the cellars of the houses, extend much deeper below the surface, and in one case the excavations are so extensive as to give comfortable shelter to more than a company of men. The rooms lead one from the other, possessing doors and lined with wood, and often containing beds. Such positions are ours now, and the Hun is out in trenches, as comfortless as ours have been.

The little villages of La Boiselle and Ovillers were built on the crest of two adjacent ridges, and a pleasant valley ran between them.

They had been visible to each other from the first streak of dawn to the last ray of light from the passing day, when the little twinkling lights from cottage window blinked and beckoned to each other in the quiet of the evening. Now, rugged ground, pitted by great shell-holes, heaps of brick and stone, snags of wire, and parts of deep trenches, are all that is left, not even ruins remain. But for the map one would not have known that villages possessing churches, stood here so short a time ago. Every building has been battered back into the soil.

To many of the dug-outs, and their original occupants, had come a blasting shell, forcing the parapet on to the mouth of the entrance, burying the men. Knowing the cost to us, it gave us a grim satisfaction to see so much evidence of German casualties, boots and clothing jutting out from chalk parapet, but greatest evidence and most easily remembered, the stench rising up from those blown-in dug-outs and all that ground about. The sun was hot, and it seemed to focus on those gleaming white trenches.

It is the battalion's turn to go up and occupy the most forward position, and continue the chipping process of attack, Sorties made by a platoon or company. We move up by way of an old German communication trench, littered with equipment of both British and Hun, the trench dips down into the valley, past a little torn wood then rises to the further slope, down again and by the entrance of an old Bosche dressing station, and about the place hangs that indescribable odour of the Hun animal, with a faint mixing of iodine and lint, for our R.A.M.C. have now taken over the place. Beyond here the trench becomes more battered and broken.

Near Achicourt, Frenchwomen working in their gardens by moonlight within 2,000 yds of the German Lines.

Remains of Church. Agny.

Old scenes, so familiar to this active pushing warfare, come back again, with almost a sense of sickness. There is no order of line; the men supporting those in front are tucked away in odd bits of trenches, and some must be passed through on the way up, and these men have scooped out little hollow places in the side, unsafe shelters, but somewhere to sleep and rest, out of the way of the feet of the men, fatigues and relief, that so often pass up and down the narrow trench.

Our guns were preparing ground for another attack, shells tearing into the soil, and bursting with great fury whine over our heads continually. How they thump the earth and beyond the brown upturned soil is blotted out by the low-lying smoke, and fumes from the shells.

There is one out there who refuses to stand such treatment, and from out the smoke, escaping blasting shell and flying metal, a big black dog, possessed with exceptional sagacity, comes bounding over the uneven ground, leaping down into our trench, as though he knew just where to find us, and that this was the shortest way out of hell. Dogs have a special liking for soldiers, and this one is quickly friends with one of our men, who promptly begins to share rations with him, thereby explaining the basis of the affection of dogs for troops. The man discovers that the animal is not hungry, but has a great thirst, as everyone had there in those hot days with the nearest source of water supply nearly two miles back, and often a barrage to pass through on the way up or going down. But he gives the dog all the water he needs. Through the remainder of the heavy shelling he sleeps snugly, curled up in the man's scooped out resting-place, who thinks he is going to have at least one prisoner to take back.

The noise of the guns has lessened, and the dog awakes, slips out into the trench to stretch and yawn, looks around and with a bound is up on to the parapet and away back to find out how his Hun friends have fared.

VOLUME V

Ralph's narrative recommences around the third week in August 1916, when the Battalion occupied trenches at Agny, south of Arras. According to the Battalion War Diary, the intervening two weeks after leaving the Somme had been spent receiving new drafts and taking part in many parades at brigade level. The most notable of these was an inspection of 36th Brigade by H.M. the King, accompanied by the Prince of Wales, which goes unrecorded by Ralph.[102]

From the 21st August until the 26th September they were rotated in and out of front line trenches at Agny, which at this point in the War was a quiet part of the line. Typical entries from the Battalion War Diary during this period state simply 'Very quiet day. Casualties nil', which was in complete contrast to the previous seven weeks spent in action in the battle of the Somme. Ralph says there could be few 'less objectionable' sectors on the whole front, but even somewhere so quiet could induce inexplicable fear or 'wind up' for no apparent reason.[103] Perhaps this fear was the inevitable result of the trauma of the Somme experience, a form of what was known during the Great War as shell-shock.

However, this respite was soon over and at the end of September the Battalion was on the move again. An entry in the Battalion War Diary for the 28th and 29th September briefly mentions the journey; Ralph's account provides the detail. He describes the novelty of being transported in French buses, which the men found highly entertaining, the long march to the camp at the Pommier Redoubt near Mametz and the realization that they had arrived back in the Somme, where the fighting continued.

After the losses suffered during the summer of 1916 the British did not have the capacity to launch further full-scale attacks. Instead, at this point they were concentrating on focused attacks on smaller sections of the German lines, where they may have some chance of success with the tactic of what was called 'Bite and Hold'. While gradually pressing forward, resisting fierce counter-attacks, the aim was to move the front line to more advantageous positions on higher ground.

Because of the intense fighting during the summer the condition of the country was appalling. Hardly a foot had not been ploughed up by shelling and on top of this came heavy rainfall, which turned the Somme chalk into sticky, clinging mud. Horses, men, limbers and lorries became stuck in the mud; the roads, such as they were, were practically impassable due to dead men, mules and horses.[104]

---

[102] WSRO RSR MSS/7/11: 10 August 1916.
[103] WSRO RSR MSS/7/11: 21 August-26 September 1916; WSRO Add. Mss. 25006: 175.
[104] Rutter [n.d.]: 104-105.

It was in these conditions that the 7th Royal Sussex Regiment started their third tour of duty in the Battle of the Somme. Moving up to the support line at Flers on the night of October 1st they endured an extremely difficult relief, which the War Diary understatedly describes as 'slow'. However, Ralph's account recalls the experience as an assault on all the senses; the stench of fumes from shells and rotting flesh, the deafening noise of heavy guns, the blinding flashes of explosives, the exhausting mud, the cold and drizzle, the dark, the confusion, bewilderment and fear. This was followed by relief when daylight broke. But daylight also revealed the extent to which the landscape had been laid to waste.

From the 3rd to the 6th October the Battalion was in front line trenches and then moved back to support. According to the Battalion War Diary, every day the shelling was intense. The German gunners knew the exact position of the trenches and losses were very heavy, although they were not involved in any actual fighting. On 7th October a previously postponed attack against Bayonet Trench took place and since the Battalion was in support, they were sent forward in readiness to move into the front line. However because of intense German resistance the assaulting troops were prevented from reaching their objectives, the 7th Royal Sussex were unable to reach their own front line and the attack was unsuccessful. Casualties from the 1st to the 8th October amounted to 7 officers and 175 other ranks, killed or wounded.[105]

Relieved on the 10th October, the Battalion moved back to a camp in Bernafay Wood, but they were kept busy with working parties and kept awake by the close proximity to British artillery. When the Battalion went back into the reserve line at Flers-Guedecourt on the 17th October a further attack against Bayonet Trench was underway, but broke down because of enemy machine gun fire and uncut wire. The attack was to be continued the following day, with the 7th Royal Sussex going into action. This was supposed to be a surprise attack, but it quickly became clear that the Germans were holding the position strongly in anticipation of an attack, so it was abandoned and the assaulting troops were withdrawn. The action that took place between the 1st and 18th October later became known as the Battle of Transloy. In the afternoon of the 19th October the 7th Royal Sussex were relieved and moved back to Mametz Wood camp; their participation in the Somme campaign was over.[106] The fighting continued for another month and finally ended on the 18th November, as a result of the appalling weather and conditions.

Ralph's account of this period, which is broadly chronological, provides some of the most detailed and vivid text in the memoir. For Ralph, the landscape is his overriding interest; he views it both as an artist and as an artillery observer and employs words to evoke what he sees. The devastation of the countryside he witnesses on the Somme in

---

[105] WSRO RSR MSS/7/11: 1-8 October 1916; Rutter [n.d.]: 106.
[106] WSRO RSR MSS/7/11: 17 October; Rutter [n.d.]: 107.

October 1916 shocks and saddens him, but at the same time, beyond the German lines, he sees a glimpse of green – a ray of hope in a shattered landscape. Passing through the same area a year later Ralph witnesses the regenerative power of nature. Shell holes and trenches are covered in a profusion of wild flowers and butterflies have colonized this previously barren landscape. Again, the regenerative power of nature stirs an almost religious fervour in Ralph and he feels it is nothing short of a miracle, bringing hope for the future.[107]

As a record of how the Great War was experienced by the men who fought, the memoir provides a rich source of evidence. The official records like the Battalion War Diary and the regimental history provide an outline of what happened, when and where. Personal testimony tells the story of what it was like to actually be there and so complements the official sources with an individual viewpoint and personal responses. It is often the mundane routine of life in the infantry that Ralph writes about; the fatigues, the working parties, the long marches and the difficulty of performing even the simplest tasks in the dark and confusion of the trenches. He praises the endurance of the men who struggled through the mud and wreckage to collect rations for their comrades in the front line, constantly in danger from artillery fire.

During this period the 7th Royal Sussex suffered heavy casualties and many of Ralph's comrades were killed or wounded. On several occasions he pays tribute to the stretcher-bearers who brought the wounded men back over almost impassable ground, while continually under fire. He describes how amid the chaos a burial party, led by a padre, paid their last respects to their comrades, and despite being shelled did not flinch until the last prayers were uttered. Other men suffered from shell-shock, which for Ralph was almost harder to witness than physical wounds. These were the realities of the war for the vast numbers of men who fought in the infantry and it is in accounts like Ralph's that their experiences are preserved.

During their brief rest at the camp at Bernafay Wood in mid October, Ralph witnessed the continued attack at Flers; the waves of infantry emerging from the trenches and coming under fire, the wounded limping back, the stretcher-bearers working tirelessly to bring back the injured and then being hit themselves. It is a bird's eye view of a battle that gives a suggestion of the experience, but from a distance. In his memoir Ralph never actually describes the experience of fighting or of killing, because fortunately, due to circumstances beyond his control, he never had to go over the top; this perhaps accounts for his survival.

The British army first used its newest weapon, the tank, in September 1916 during the attack on Flers-Courcelett. In October Ralph records seeing them, 'resembling great toads, squatting in the centre of the track'. Writing home to his parents on 23rd October,

---

[107] WSRO Add. Mss. 25006: 187, 189.

he says they are 'weird things' that 'glide along and resemble a whale or some prehistoric monster', which must have given the Germans 'Cold Feet'. However, Ralph's pencil sketch of two tanks is probably more helpful than his description.[108] He does acknowledge the limitations of the new weapons in battle, as well as the vulnerability of their crews.

For the last ten days of October the 7th Royal Sussex were in rest, albeit in very poor conditions, but Ralph describes how the men soon made the best of it, scavenging for available materials to improve their comfort. On 1st November the Battalion moved back into the quiet trenches at Agny, south of Arras, where they had been in the late summer. During November and December they rotated in and out of the line, alternating fatigues and working parties with parades, training and cleaning up.

A week before Christmas orders came through for Ralph to leave the 7th Royal Sussex, but he doesn't say why. In the manuscript version Ralph remembers receiving the news with glee – like a schoolboy going home for the holidays – tinged with some regret at leaving the Battalion. In the 1948 revised version he explains the reason and recalls declining the offer of a commission. However, a few days later the commanding officer, Col. A.J. Sansom, informed him it was an order. Ralph speaks of his regret at leaving the men with whom he had served for so long and he pays tribute to the bravery and comradeship of the many who had died or had been wounded.[109] As a postscript to this phase of his time in the army, he gives a resume of the subsequent movements of the 7th Royal Sussex, accompanied by a sketch of Harold, the regimental mascot who is mentioned in one of Ralph's letters to his sister.[110]

Casualties among junior officers in the Great War were disproportionately high; 17% died compared with 12% of soldiers in the ranks. During the bloodiest phases of fighting six weeks was the average length of time they could expect to survive, which was in part due to the practice in the British army of junior officers leading their men into battle and on sorties and raids into no man's land. The heavy casualties sustained in the major offensives of 1915 and 1916 led to a shortage of junior officers and increasingly, non-commissioned officers were promoted from the ranks to fill the gaps.[111]

Men like Ralph, who had valuable experience both of trench warfare and of leadership were often selected for training and commissioned as 'Temporary 2nd Lieutenants'. Earlier in the war officers were almost exclusively drawn from the upper echelons of British society. However, as men from the ranks were promoted the social mix became more varied and the term 'Temporary Gentlemen' was coined, suggesting not only the

---

[108] WSRO Add. Mss. 25006: 192, 199, 205; Appendix, p. 273.
[109] WSRO Add. Mss. 25001: 145; WSRO Add. Mss. 25006: 209.
[110] WSRO Add. Mss. 25006: 210; Appendix, p. 259.
[111] Lewis-Stempel (2010).

April, 1917.

**Ralph Ellis in the uniform of
2nd Lieut, The Queen's (Royal West Surrey) Regiment**

temporary nature of the commission, but also the temporary elevation in social class. This could be a hazardous situation for new officers to negotiate in the Mess.

After a short period of leave, on the 3rd January 1917 Ralph commenced training at the 9th Officers' Cadet Battalion Camp at Gailes, Ayreshire[112] and was gazetted as a Temporary 2nd Lieutenant to the 2nd Queen's (Royal West Surrey) Regiment on the 26th April.[113] He returned to France at the end of May and having passed through the notorious 'Bull Ring' base camp at Étaples, on the 18th June he was pleased to join the 2nd Queen's at Courcelles, where they were resting after being involved in action at Bullecourt in May.

By the end of June the 2nd Queen's were in trenches at Hendecourt near Bullecourt. During July and the first week of August they rotated in out of the front line, encountering moderate shelling, bombing and sniping activity and undertaking fatigues, working parties and patrols in no man's land. Interspersed with these duties were periods of rest and training.[114]

After a few weeks with 'B' Company, Ralph was appointed Intelligence Officer, a role he was well suited to. The British occupied a portion of what was the heavily fortified German Hindenburg Line, which had been captured by Australian troops in May. For once they had the advantage of being on higher ground, which was perfect for the purposes of observation. Working with the artillery gunners, machine gunners, trench mortars and snipers, Ralph directed their fire and helped to 'worry' the Germans. Two particular incidents stand out in Ralph's memory from this time: one was the destruction by the heavy artillery of two 'Mebus', (reinforced concrete German pill-boxes) named Gog and Magog,[115] and the other concerned accurate and deadly German snipers, who were eventually 'quietened'. Both these incidents were revised and rewritten in the 1948 version of the memoir.[116]

After being relieved on 7th August, the 2nd Queen's moved into a period of intense training behind the lines before starting their journey north to join the offensive known as the Third Battle of Ypres or Passchendaele, which had started on the 31st July. Arriving in the area behind Ypres on the 29th August, they did not go into action until October, by which time the offensive had stalled and descended into attritional fighting, at enormous cost in casualties to both sides. Furthermore, bad weather in October made the battlefield an impossible quagmire. On both occasions that the 2nd Queen's were involved in attacks they were not successful and they sustained heavy casualties.

---

[112] TNA WO339/83413.
[113] *The London Gazette*, 12 May 1917.
[114] 2nd Battalion, The Queen's (Royal West Surrey) Regiment War Diary
[115] WSRO Add. Mss. 25006: 231.
[116] WSRO Add. Mss. 25001: 147-149.

However, Ralph was not with them. According to the 2nd Queen's War Diary, on 27th August an advance party consisting of Transport Officer 2nd Lieut. Perry and Intelligence Officer 2nd Lieut. Ellis went ahead with others from the division to reconnoitre at Ypres.[117] His officer service record states that he was wounded in his forearm and elbow on 30th August near Ypres. Now it was Ralph's turn to become a casualty and be taken back down the line through all the stages of the 'Chain of Evacuation'. Ralph had a 'Blighty' wound – this was the end of his 'march with the infantry'.[118]

In his memoir Ralph only gives his injury the briefest of mentions – a mere three lines, and there the final volume ends. In the 1948 revised text he gives a little more detail:

> 'No pain, but a swift transition from strength to weakness. My companion, whose name I did not know, or see again, quickly removed the strap from his field glasses and applied a tourniquet, which saved the situation and made off towards the Menin Road for assistance. Shortly afterwards another piece of metal buried itself in the earth close by my feet. This had a stimulating effect upon me. With the assistance of a corporal who came that way, I was led off in another direction until we came to a Battery of our Artillery, faces dimly seen, a sip of water and a stretcher party and so continued my journey by various means of transport, the most restful of which perhaps was the horse drawn ambulance to a Base Hospital and some time later on to England.
>
> It was at the casualty clearing station that the resident Padre came to me and asked for my home address, and also to tell me, with a smile, that I should not return to Active Service – I discovered that this information did not give me the pleasure he anticipated but a genuine regret that I could no longer march on with the infantry.'[119]

---

[117] 2nd Battalion, The Queen's (Royal West Surrey) Regiment War Diary: 27 August 1917.
[118] TNA WO339/83413.
[119] WSRO Add. Mss. 25001: 150-151.

Achicourt, although as near to the line as Agny, because of its low situation, was still occupied by a civilian population, as well as by troops that rest here in reserve, and our gun pits were in the fields about it. Yet through being in such proximity to the line, the people are unable to move about freely during the day. The shops and estaminets open after dark, and the women folk may be seen working in the gardens as the daylight is fading away, or by the soft light of the moon.

This was a phase of war carried out under the most favourable conditions possible, not even patrolling at night beyond the front line gave a greater excitement than is usually obtained in creeping along over a half seen, unknown ground, through rank dew laden grass, in deep shell-holes, or by the Arras-Bapaume road, which passed straightly through the lines and between was littered with wire, great limbs and branches of trees that had grown up stately on either side, and now were splintered and bare. Picking one's way noiselessly from tree to tree, listening and hearing only the cough of a Bosch sentry in his trench, or sap head, the distant rumble of his transport, coming right up into Beaurains, on the battered outskirts of which was his foremost line. The noise of our own limbers, bringing our rations up to Agny, seeing too the flickering flash of Machine gun, sweeping the ground in a swift, far reaching arc.

To the average individual fear must at some time or other grip one tightly. Few can pass through without one or two vivid experiences of acute "wind up". Yet this was the last place to expect such an experience.

A communication trench, not used a great deal, before it reached our support line, crossed over the Arras-Bapaume road, which at this spot was cut below the level of the ground. Therefore the trench sloped down into it and ran across the road between high barricades, a deeply dug shelter had been excavated beneath the road on the left side, which sometimes accommodated a gunner forward observation officer, his orderly and signaller, for the high bank of the road, between the big splintered elm trees, gave a good view of the Hun front line, 800 yards away on the further ridge.

Agny

Often one had to pass this way, visiting O-pips and sniping posts, and at night to follow the road, a short cut to our front line and the ground beyond. But there was nothing to account for the extraordinary distaste one felt to pass this spot. Before reaching it, wherever one's thoughts had been, they immediately focussed about that dip in the trench, and gave one an almost overwhelming desire to avoid passing; and, forcing oneself to, a powerful urgency possessed one to rush past, to fly from it with all the strength of one's limbs. It gave one the most acute sense of "wind-up" experienced and uncanny because so altogether unexplainable.

If our casualties were few, the Huns probably were light also, though our trench mortars sometimes hammered his line and with rifle we occasionally caught a careless Bosche exposing himself on the steep bank of the railway cutting.
The distance between the lines in most places was too great for accurate shooting, but firing once at a pin-point of pink, a Hun face, watching the burst of his spiteful little fish-tail bombs, failed to score, the owner withdrew his face and was careful not to give an opportunity for a second shot, but amused himself by signalling with hat raised on stick, a "wash-out", as we do on the range, when a shot goes wide.
We came to like this quiet spot. Few sectors could be less objectionable on the whole front, but we had to leave it at the end of September 1916.

Agny – Achicourt Road.

Flers and Guedecourt October 1916.

Little time was spent in getting back to the Somme once more. Our own motor lorries carried us part of the way, then dumped us by the roadside and left us to be fell upon by a storm of rain before billets could be found. Most of the barns of the village were filled with the freshly gathered grain; the rain drove some of us to find our own shelter, which we did, tucking ourselves away in the farm waggons, and the cart-sheds, from which scurried the fowls in frantic alarm.

The following day the French conveyed us the remainder of the way, and their conveyances are greatly to be preferred to our own motor lorries, in which troops are dumped with less concern than is given to unperishable goods. The French lorries contain seats, and one travels in almost comfort. The drivers are a mixed lot, ranging from smart young mechanics, probably unfit in some way for more active service; to fat, grey-haired Frenchmen, made more rotund by the quantity of clothing they appear to wear. Many of the drivers are negroes, picturesque figures some of them, wearing big black fur coats, and their equally black faces surmounted by the light blue French chapeau. They speed us on our way much more swiftly than their railroad. We are like boys being driven to a school treat, singing and finding great amusement as we are jolted along through town and village, by roads bordered by apple trees, loaded with fruit. We take our share of them and laugh at the men who must run like hares to catch up their lorry. Some ahead break down and await the last lorry containing spare parts and a swift working mechanic, who quickly puts the gear in order again. But we laugh at the occupants as we rush past them. It is a great life, and good to enjoy it while you may. To watch the country, slipping away on either side; batches of prisoners improving the state of the roads, who stare at us stolidly in passing, whilst one or two guessing at our destination, smile cunningly.

The pleasure of the journey is left behind with the French lorries. No need to ask where we are.

The appearance of the country in the distance, and the busy nature of the traffic on the road, shouts again of the Somme.

We are formed up, and march away into the night. Rain has fallen, which the amount of traffic has made much of, turning the surface of the road into a thin slush. The air is raw and cold, the pack weighs heavily on the shoulders, one suddenly becomes aware of these, and other unpleasant details, which together acts like a drop-curtain; shutting out all light, warmth and rest, and dragging our day far into the long night. Fortunately, we do not know the length of the march ahead of us, or the momentary spasm of depression might be of longer duration. Each cluster of houses we pass that at first show some signs of stability, we imagine may be our resting place for the night. But we pass them by, and envy the troops that crowd the sides of the road, and look as though they had but recently come from the line, and by their numbers must be crowded into every available space in these decrepit, stale looking houses. But the light of a candle, and the flickering flare of a wood fire, about which are clustered bunches of cheerful men, looks inviting enough to us. A halt is made at the railway crossing, and trucks, filled with lightly wounded troops pass by. They feel that the laugh is on their side just now, and make the most of it. After this darkness seems to settle about us, and the way becomes more desolate. We are over the old trench system, past what had been villages, battered out of all recognition. The big motor lorries which share with us the new-made road, tower above the dark zig-zag outline of remaining brickwork and hummocks of earth on either side. Beyond the crest of this ridge, the country opens out again, a darker plane against the night sky, and it is as though this portion of the earth had tried to reflect the stars of the heaven, so many were the lights that on all sides told of the hugh camp we could not see. It was a great and cheering sight, as though no one cared for the enemy, such a few kilometres ahead.

It made us feel suddenly less tired of the march and somewhere in the darkness made more intense by these points of light is the Pommiere Redoubt, where we are to camp. At last we strike it, stumbling along dog-tired, a voice cries out, "Who are you"? and answer "Sussex". Our regard for the Commander of the Brigade is increased a good deal when we see that it is he who has finally guided us to the Camp. A few tents and some bivouacs on a knoll of ground, sufficient to accommodate about half the battalion, the remainder, after efforts to crowd them all into bivy or tents are finally distributed into the deep trenches, the defences of this old strong point. They curse profusely at such varied accommodation, but the old soldier gets to work at once, "Scrounges" round for corrugated iron sheeting, remains of old dug-outs, or anything else that may make a shelter over the trench. Beneath this they bunch together for warmth, and sleep.

Daybreak found us encamped on high ground, everywhere around were camps of men crowded together in tent and bivouac and old trench. Horse and transport lines made dark splashes against the soil of that old shelled ground, while the road near by bore a continuous stream of motor lorries "bun carts", limbers and the odd bits of war traffic, the staff car, motor cycle of the dispatch rider and an occasional bunch of prisoners coming down to the "cage" near to our camp. Long lines of horses and mules that in the distance are like hugh black snakes winding their way in and out of the camps and dumps, laden with shells for the forward dumps, near to the guns; and towards dusk with rations and water for the infantry. Owing to the heavy, broken nature of the ground it is the surest way of getting the stuff up, but hard, strenuous work for the animals.
It is a most exhilarating scene at first, but after many days spent here and a few of them at the hub or culminating point of all this motion the sight depresses, one hungers to get away from it.

Pommiere Redoubt.

The Summer of 1916 was cut short early by cold and wet weather. Such conditions added to this natureless country made a very winter of it. There was no intermediate stage of a mellow autumn. We had marched out of a land richly dressed in summer garb, well-worn perhaps, with a hint of change in its colouring, but perfect, when compared to the shorn wintry look of this land, we had come to.

On the road up to the line we met men who had pushed forward our position to its furthermost point, the fight had gone well with them, and when their objective had been reached, had left it for others and ourselves to hold on to. So in passing spoke emphatically of the discomforture of the Huns and the ease with which the line was held. They "had knocked the stuffin out of the Hun". Thus men speak after a successful fight, and when they are leaving the line.

On a quiet front where a large sector is occupied by one division, the roads up to the line carry a traffic as familiar because of the well-known distinguishing marks of each unit, as the vehicles which pass up and down the streets of one's own county town or village, but here the traffic was as unfamiliar and as plentiful as that which is seen in the heart of a great city.

This ground had been fought for almost foot by foot, only the indispensable roads had been restored, nature had'nt a chance, and the roads and tracks lay across the country in broad bands plain to see, nothing hid them except the contours of the ground, everything else was levelled. Our heavy guns found slight shelter amongst the hummocks of torn earth and rubble, and splintered tree, all that remained of the villages.

Darkness settles over the earth increasing and hiding all movement, but still away ahead are many little points of light stabbing the darkness, home of the gunner. We pass on over the sheltering ridge and the road becomes a part of the other shelled ground, its surface churned into a thick mass which tires the feet, partially fills the shell hole and covers the dead mules.

The Observation Baloons from Bernafay Camp.

The darkness hides much, but in such a place that intense nauseating smell, combination of fumes from H.E. shells and rotting flesh, — the odour of blood and iron. This is sufficient to direct one to the front.

The last of our heavies is past, head down, slogging along the foul track, the wall of blackness on our left is suddenly split open discharging a volume of noise and flame, so near that for a second the eyes are blinded by the violent intensity of the flash and the senses are numbed by the force of the discharge. The momentary impression is that a shell has burst right in our midst. The platoon wakes up, sort of feels round to find out if one is still whole, curses the gunner, laughs and settles down once more to the dogged endurance of the march, all in about the same space of time that it has taken that 4.5 howitzer shell to go romping away over to the Hun reliefs coming up to the line.

The long file of men emerge one after the other from the length of trench that has sheltered almost the last lap of their journey across a higher level of ground. A favourite night resort for Hun heavies, and stike a narrow lane.

Out of the groping darkness made more intense by high banks enclosing the road, emerge other figures whom we are to releive, and our men are pouring in, mingle and quickly form a jostling crowd, a movement of dark masses, of shapes without form. The black night wipes out all detail, every distinguishing mark, figures surge up and down, bewildered and cursing, scarcely avoiding the half a dozen stretcher cases waiting to be carried further back, but their is no hope of evacuating them whilst the releif is in progress, so they lie and wait in the cold and drizzle of rain, and cry out feebly in their weakness to all these men who stumble against the stretchers before being aware of their presence. Long files of other men loaded and almost as tired as the men they releive pour in and follow the little sunken road for a short distance, then turn right and strike out into the open to go on beyond to occupy the front line.

These passing men add to the confusion in that confined space, but discipline drills into the mind the desire for order.

The thick noise of feet squelching in the slick mud is punctuated by sharp orders from N.C.O's, and the men to be relieved gather together quickly with much soft cursing and pulling at their more bewildered comrades, line up and move off.

Arriving at a strange part of the line in the midst of darkness one awaits the light and welcomes it with great keenness, until then one feels almost blindfolded, without any sure knowledge of position, darkness delights to distort all things and confuse the mind with its impenetrable vagueness, so one welcomes the sane, unimaginative day which puts an end to the black mystery of night.

Daylight came and pointed out to us first how that shell had burst a little further from us than we thought, but near enough to send the men resting in the scooped out hollows at the top of the bank scurrying to the bottom, there to stay for the remainder of the night, squatting with back to the earth and waterproof sheet flung over their heads.

The little lane we held crossed a wave of ground, dipped into the hollow, rose to the next and into Flers. This section of it spoke of the short stay of the Huns on this line. On the left bank but two dugouts had been finished, an Officers', made comfortable with chairs from the village and the signallers' one of whom remains, — for burial, — The other bank had been scooped out too by our own men before pushing on to the line we then held. Of the village itself nothing remained whole. Splintered timber and the wreckage of houses littered the ground. The Bosche artillery as though wrought to a high pitch of spitefulness at having lost it worried the place daily with shrapnel and H.E. adding if possible to its chaotic condition and making our little trips there for water, timber, and the dump of sand bags a trifle hurried.

Daylight pointed out these things and that we were almost at the furthest reach of this dead brown land. Oh this truly God forsaken country, burnt bare of life, that familiarity can never breed in one a real unfeeling regard for. In the advance we have made through this land our forerunner had been a scorching flame, licking the earth to brown ashes, striking down every tree, not even a bush remains whole, and now with diabolical thoroughness the Hun gunners seek out the few remaining patches of green verdure, a cluster of splintered trees about the remains of a humble building, not entirely destroyed, driving back into the dark earth these few signs of a prosperous land.

Flers had been sheltered by many trees, they had encircled it and on one side a green slope had run up to meet their shade. This had been a fertile spot where the villagers had grown their vegetables; one small patch remained, and against the surrounding drab browns, these growing things were a mingling of bright greens and yellows, and a little summer house was there almost untouched. These too disappeared, heavy shells whined over our heads, rushed down into the earth and tore it to pieces with appalling violence, so they methodically searched up and down that further slope of ground stamping out every vestige of growing life, turning a fair land into stark desolation. Not a smile in the landscape? Yes, beyond the Hun line we catch a glimpse of a land green and beautiful with banks of trees still a mass of foliage, this brooding barrenness of brown desolation makes that glimpse of beauty stand out like the sudden vision of a glorious future, but it is a most depressing thought to think that all our progress must be made at such a cost, behind a scorching flame, scarring all things with such brutal thoroughness. How long must it so remain? The question is answered in less than 12 months. One passed that way and saw.

Flers

Although the trees were still no more than gaunt grotesque shapes, even they had leaves that tried to cover their deformities. But the ground itself, never had one seen such colour, such perfect planning, nature had leapt back to her tortured naked earth with all the abandoned love and sympathy of a mother, and clothed it as never it had been so luxuriantly and fitly clothed. Shell holes and trenches were entirely hidden beneath a prolific growth of green grasses, and this formed merely a setting for every specie of wild flower this land knew. There were wonderful and separate schemes of colouring. Here, great masses of small white flowers heaped together like a bridal wreath about this ground, newly won. Then nature clapped her hands, laughed, and the scheme changed, tall yellow flowers gained the day, ran a riot over the hummocks of earth, bent to the light breeze and shook their golden heads in the sun light, studded with gold the purple patches of thistle and the little gardens of less brightly hued flowers. Then as though she had remembered suddenly how all this land had been bought, came laden with deep red poppies, massed them together, and let them dribble out into the green like the blood that had been so freely spilt here. Over all these flowers dancing in the sunlight were many butterflies, the bold swift Brimstone, gay Painted lady, Swallowtail, aristocrat and leader of fashion with many others of much lesser degree. These spent their days in faintly kissing as many of the numberless flowers as they could.

Oh! this was a land changed into a garden, beautifully and greatly planned, a master gardener had worked a miracle of wonder, created a garland of splendid memory over this soil and wrote boldly across its surface a promise of a great future in wealth and fruitfulness it had not known before.

Now the way of the Infantry goes out beyond all the other units of War, but one came to have a great regard for the endurance of others, in these days when great shells and bombs sought out the guns, parks and camps, roads and tracks that led up to the Front. There was this track by which we had come. Following that little valley, then rounding a swell of ground, came within view of that far ridge of green.

It was almost daybreak. We came to collect the rations which should be dumped here by our limbers, but found the track close packed with guns, limbers loaded with shells and G.S. wagons, all held up by two four inch guns who had attempted to turn up into a position by Flers, but instead plunged deeply into mud up to the axle, and were held there fast. All about them is deep mud. The track is thick with it and made foul by the bodies of mules and horses struck down by the shrapnel that arrives like winged devils and bursts suddenly over this way.

The light is creeping slowly but surely up into the sky, dissolving the night, yet the riders sit almost motionless and stoically on those mud splashed, and hard worked horses and mules. Further back, unable to move forward for the press in front we find our own limbers and fuming quarter-master Sergeants mightily anxious to hand over the sand bags filled with rations and to get away out of this rotting mire over which with the increasing light hangs heavy the ominous threat of blasting shell fire. The men are given their two bags or two cans of water and told to get back. They know the track and pick their way through the deep ruts of mud, brushing past mud clogged wheels and steaming straining horses that are just beginning to disentangle themselves and move back the other way from this ill-omened spot. The eyes search the further end of the valley and see that it is still cloaked in mist.

We hurry on, for further forward is much safer than this spot will be if that veil of mist is lifted before this traffic is clear away. Turning to the right up a little narrow sunken lane, we pass a battery of howitzers, morticed into the bank, then strike out hurriedly across the open, picking our way between the shell holes, some are new and have approached very near to that battery, and some are full of 18 pounder shells carried there at night on the backs of mules, pannier fashion and dumped in great haste as we advanced even before the guns arrived.

This too is the way of the stretcher bearers that all day and all night traverse it with the wounded. Two returning with empty stretcher have been torn and flung brutally into these shell holes. Heavy shells visit here at any old time, targets abound, the ground is burdened with our guns and supporting infantry, dumped into bits of crumbling trenches, bereft of any vestige of comfort and well worn tracks used much by night and often by day.

Leaving our support line in the lane and following again that dip in the ground we keep well to the right where the ground rises suddenly and take what shelter it can give, which is more imaginary than real. You cannot mistake the way, it is marked by the crumpled forms of those who first advanced with the tanks and by those who since hurried along the track. Many tanks became casualties too. We pass one, hit squarely, torn open and the interior gives forth a burnt nauseating smell which one turns from as a sensitive animal springs away from a breath of air bearing the hint of blood of its own kind.

The Hun may watch plainly every little group or solitary runner crossing the open valley at this point as all must to get to the line or away from it, and his field gunners miss few opportunities.

Tanks coming out of action.

A stretcher party passes slowly, making its way back and leading one or two walking wounded, one is full of admiration for these men who pass up and down that hellish bit of ground. There was Bridger and others of our own stretcher bearers who did so constantly during the time we occupied the line, some escaped, others did not, but all walked in the fear of those swift shells that knew to a yard the way we must go.

Arriving at the other side, a few yards from the roughly dug trench that winds up on to the ridge and the firing line, feel that we are in luck, but the thought comes too swiftly, a voice shouts out "Which way to Battalion headquarters"? The direction is given to the three runners emerging from a trench a little lower down. The last word is scarcely out of the mouth when it is caught up by the swift fierce rush of a shell and is carried into the midst of those men with a hellish frenzied burst of splitting metal. One shriek of dreadful terror and three more mark the path of the infantry.

The trench as it crests the ridge almost ceases to exist and there are lengths of it that run at right angles to the Hun position. He knows it well for he dug it.

The men we met on the road who had won this line spoke of the ease with which it was held, they were right, but that was before the Hun gunners had found time to take up new positions and register on to our lines. Now they play a pretty game, with many shells including the little whizz-bangs that zipped and burst up and down that shallow gulley, tumbling the earth into it and men too, some lay half buried in the soil at the bottom, and men passing hurriedly up or down have worn holes in the sides of the bank where their feet have momentarily and forcefully rested, skipping with long strides to avoid the huddled up forms as one would spring from side to side of a path to avoid a patch of mud or pool of water.

Evening in support S. of Agny

No one lingers here except pain and death and one dazed fellow who crouches beneath the shelter of a jagged sheet of corrugated iron refusing to move up into the line or further down out of it, paralysed with fear he heeds neither proffered help or order, but is like a weak animal hypnotised by the accurate advent of these little screaming shells that seem to follow one up and down the trench and across that valley with devilish persistency. With luck one passed scatheless but all if they dare to think of these must have great doubts of emerging untouched.

One man whether he were fool or hero filled one with much admiration, walking so slowly and with greatest unconcern just as one would stroll by lovely pathways with nothing further to do than enjoy the pageant of a summer's day.

All others hastened along the straight parts of the trench, halting and resting only where it was deeper and not infiladed.

The front line was in a little better condition, but the shelling was constant and accurate, and the men spent much of their time in digging one another out from beneath blown in parapet. Casualties were many. Cheeseman, D.C.M. and many others left us here. A few came down with every bit of manhood shaken out of them, shell shock cases in the first throes of their stricken state are not nice to see. It is easier to look on wounds than those you have known as men with all the spirit that makes a man, gone, lost grip of, it is the most pitiful sight that a pitiless war can show.

The stretcher cases came down frequently, requiring relays of bearers to carry them back. Some with slight wounds walking down were hit again. These and others seldom went further than the forward dressing station.

By the side of the track we buried some, as we like to with high regard and honour when time and place allow.

A grey sky kept mournful watch over the dark dead earth, whilst a few hundred yards away heavy black smoke surges up continuously, moves from place to place, draws nearer, and with the roar of each bursting shell makes a fit setting for such a burial.

The Curé's garden Agny.

The grave is dug and the physical remains of three heavily built men are carried across the muddy slippery ground and lowered with what care we may into the pit. The padre arrives and the men who have dug stand by with head bowed whilst the little service is held.

    Heavy shells drop nearer. The track is empty save for these few men who remain motionless, helmet in hand. Then — nearer a tearing roar and a black pall of smoke rises and floats silently past, and the air is full of the hum and whirr of flying earth and metal, one piece of shell seems to detach itself and fall hissing towards them, strikes and buries itself with appalling force into the earth not two inches from the foot of one of the men. not a man moves, the last words of the prayer are gravely uttered before cover is sought and taken.

We came back to Bernafay camp and for a day or two rested in canvas huts decorated on the outside with bold crude splashes of colour, the style affected by the camouflage artists. Not that there was much to hide, when the whole district seethed with the busy movement that took no account of bombs, often dropped during darkness, and an occasional long range shell which, coming to ground so vastly populated with men and the trappings of war, causes little disturbance.
A few men seen running, or may be half a dozen stampeding horses all spreading outwards from the burst of smoke and flying earth like the little ripples formed on a broad surface of water by a stone flung into its depth disturbing a fraction of it for a moment then quickly becomes an unruffled surface once more.

A fascinating sight this great camp, to one arriving suddenly in its midst, the whole of the British Army might seem to be encamped here, spread out over hill and vale as far as the eye can see, a host that had stripped the country bare: as a plague of locusts settles and eats up every growing thing.

The Marie, Agny used as an observation post.

Side by side were units, some such as ourselves resting away from our centre of action, whilst to others this was their firing line.

    We were always inclined to be a trifle pessimistic as to the near future when the divisional band was sent to play to us, had got into the habit of interpreting it as an indication that unpleasant work was not far ahead, so that we did not welcome it on that account, but apart from that to invite a band, however good, to compete with a couple of four inch guns is not fair to the bandsmen or to those forced to listen, and when the guns were not belching forth shells that romped away over our heads to a target in Bapaume or away beyond, there was always the clatter of horse and heavy wheels and noisy motor lorries on the road near to the camp. Things by themselves to be understood and tolerated, but set a band amongst it and the whole thing becomes a pandemonium of noise as soothing as the blare and racket of an English fair.

    So we shared our rest with the gunners work and found more amusement in watching the slick work of these men loading and firing those long guns than in listening to the bandsmans effort that was far too much out of harmony with all this earnest concentration of the business of war. In a few days its tide carried us on up again by that same busy road into the line and this time the division was to attack.

Tanks which had crawled up as far as they might with safety during the day, were passed, looming up in the semi-darkness and resembling great toads, squatting in the centre of the track. Only a few were needed in this attack which took place on a small frontage.

The earth and sky meet on the ridge from which it is possible to see a hint of buildings in Bapaume. Guidecourt is on the right. And earth and sky are melting together; grey and indistinct in the fading light.

Snipers Post on the Arras - Bapaume Road nr. Arras.

From just below the ridge emerging out of the earth figures go forward, make little short rushes and then lie down becoming one with the silent unmoving earth again.

From behind us the guns are methodically pounding away as they have done day after day. It may have increased a little in the past hour, but at the appointed second a tornado of shells are let loose, the air is loaded with their screams, in the mad race they pursue to the German position.

Up out of the earth again rise many figures. A long line of them this time, helmeted with small knapsack on back, but there is a great amount of character depicted in the way they carry rifle and bayonet. The majority sling it by the strap across the shoulder indifferent now almost as to their own fate and not over much thought for the result of the "show". It is work to be got through the same as the long march or tiring fatigue. Others lurch forward, head down, the rifle at the trail as a man pushes with determination towards his destination against a storm of wind and rain. A few slope their arms as on parade, walk up-rightly in spite of shell torn ground, head up, looking steadily before them, their bearing suggests that they see a great way beyond the immediate vileness of this little attack, its result, and whatever their own fate in the business may be, hold a vision of the higher purpose of it all.

The whole line moves forward together, but owing to the formation of the ground and its broken nature the line becomes split up into little groups and some rise to the crest of the ridge before the others, are silhouetted against the glowing sky and the rolling smoke, pass over and are gone from sight. Another line of men rise out of the earth, line up and in a similar way go forward. A matter of minutes between each wave, but in that time the Hun gunners have got to work. The smoke from their shells rises in sudden upward driven bursts from out of our position whence our men have risen, spring up again and again where the communication trench rises from the little valley.

A corner of cemetry, Agny containing graves of French soldiers killed in 1914 -1915. loopholes in wall made by Germans in defence of village against the French.

You can mark the sphere of their action across the valley and up on to the ridge, a barrier dropped too late and above the ridge are the white puffs of smoke from the bursting shrapnel and the noise of all this storm of shells intermingles, becomes a chaos of harsh throbbing sound, only the bursting shells of heavier calibre punctuated it with more forceful detonations.

Then the back-wash appears, men limping back, some making short runs, drop into shell holes, rise again, making other short rushes, scarcely daring to hope that they may get through unhit again, that belt of ground so stabbed by shells.

Two stretcher bearers are working with admirable devotion and coolness, again and again they go forward, disappear over the ridge, returning, the stretcher carried between them stumbling along in quick, jerky movements over the rough ground — down into a trench, then returning again over the open, this time but one is able to walk and carries his comrade on his back, one watches these two with absorbing anxiety, hoping that they may get through, for all about that ground they must traverse is the birth-place of little volcanic eruptions, obstructing and greatly endangering their progress. They are hidden by smoke of shell, appear again, stumbling forward with his burden in little short rushes, is almost into the trench, then overtaken by a pursuing shell coming to earth not many yards to their left. Both are hurled to the ground, the earth receives them and is still, while the night lowers its curtain over the scene.

The wounded pass by and a few prisoners, all night long the former are being passed back, running the gauntlet of bursting shell many times until the ambulance is able to receive them and awakens their slumbering wounds, in its jolting passage over the rough track back to sleep and rest.

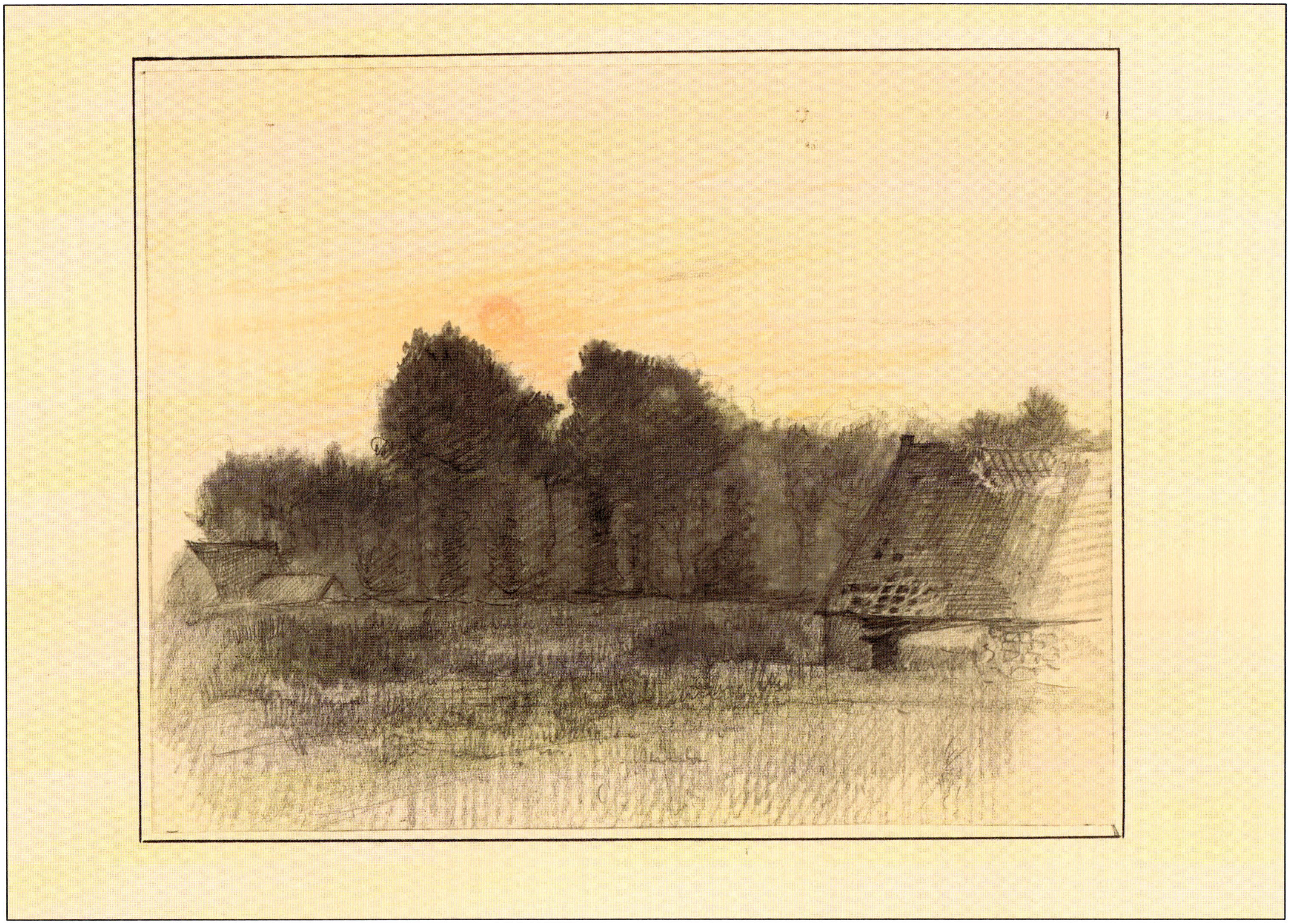

We had seen the tanks stationery, a solid looking mass of metal, but as they went up or came out of action seeing them slowly thrusting forward through the mud, nosing and feeling their way into and over deep shell holes and portions of deep trenches, there was no sense of ordinary mechanical movement. A thin whiff of blue fumes arise as breath on cold air and the thing slithers forward, like some pre-historic animal having slept through the ages and aroused by this thunder of war had thrust its way up through the crust of the earth to roam once more over the land.

The rains had made all approaches impossible to heavy traffic and further progress for the infantry over such sodden ground consequently difficult.

The Somme offensive was ended, and in this state we left it; a condition the word Somme will for ever conjure up in the minds of most men who went through the latter part of that offensive.

Before being relieved we had attempted to improve the shallow trench we occupied as all good troops should do, but the rain poured steadily down frustrating all our efforts, and owing to the little shelters which had previously been scooped out of the walls, completed the ruin. The soft earth crumbled in, often burying equipment and food, and tumbling in on to resting men.

One felt sorry for the relief who came to take over and dwell in such a ditch, taking our place as we scrambled out, glad to be clear of it and wend our way back over greasy ground by tracks swimming in thin mud or thick water whichever you cared to call it, passed and splashed from head to foot by the long line of shell laden tired looking mules, and as we watched the observation baloon high up in the air above us, rather envied those men who rise clear of all the mud and litter of war.

We push on over old battle grounds, skirting battered woods and villages, marching on through varying consistencies of mud into the darkness, which makes the track obscure and our destination difficult to find, halting by the waggon lines of gunners to ask of them the way.

Batt. H.Q. Agny.

They know as little of their neighbours in these camps as a resident in a big city can tell you of the people dwelling in the next street, but act in a neighbourly way, giving us a drink of hot tea.

This is Mametz and this black night somewhere hides our camp. At last we strike it, drawn by the blaze of the big wood fire round which others who had arrived before us stand, drying their steaming clothes, boiling water in their little mess tins and getting a little warmth and comfort into their bodies.

The camp is made up of a collection of canvas huts, most of them open at either end, and through being pitched on this high ground the cold wind screams through, quickly driving out every bit of warmth the hard march had given to the body, making one aware of wet clothing and sodden boots, but it does not take long to improve matters, to close up one end of the hut and search about in the darkness for wood and with luck find a little coke left by out-going troops, light a fire and with the precious store of tea and sugar brought with us and a couple of biscuits make a meal which, though not a feast is partaken of with keen relish and enjoyment. It gives an impetous to sleep, but the damp cold awakes us early and from then our sleep is as fitful as in the trenches.

One other short march sets us free of all this stricken earth, but not quite far enough back to provide good billets. A trench long disused is our resting place for another night, but arriving in daylight it gives us plenty of opportunity for making ourselves comfortable, searching the ground for material for making shelters and wood for a fire.

Before night overtakes us everyone has forgotten the "grouse" they had at finding themselves in such poor quarters, having expected something better after the line, but now they are settled and snug. Little gatherings of three or four men sharing a shelter which they have made together with a blaze of warmth at the entrance.

Private "Alfred"

The First Frost of winter touches us with its cold grip and wakes us early the following morning, but the air is dry and the ground firmer.

The keen enjoyment is experienced again in setting forth on a good road, and added to by the thought of leaving such a land where war runs naked.

The cards are shuffled again, we are hurried back by motor bus and come again to the quiet front by Arras, setting free another division to take up a harder task in less quiet places.

We drop once more into the routine of the old trench warfare with its cheerful accompaniment of days spent in support in occupied villages. This is war half cloaked.

From our quiet line we watch the Hun making his first preparations for leaving this front in the following spring.

A week before Christmas came orders to leave the Battalion and to proceed to England, which one did with the same glee as a school boy goes home for the holiday, but also with regrets at leaving the Battalion, half hoping that one would return again to the old Unit.

Of the original 1100 men drawn together by a spirit of high adventure and patriotism few remain. We know where many rest and in after days one met others disabled but looking forward to life and civilian occupation once more with the same pluck they displayed out there. Some may come through with no great hurt, but the Battalion marches on, its ranks filled by other men who knew it not in its younger days of inspiration and comradeship, but they carry on through many of the differing phases of the War, finally reaping the results of the work of men who also suffered, laughed and fought through the long tedious days of the first three years of War.

Subsequent movements of the 7th Batt. R. Sx. Regt.

The Battalion took part in the Arras offensive attacking on the 9th April 1917 just N of the Arras-Cambrai Rd.

Most of the summer was spent in the turbulent Monchy sector before Arras. In October they were moved back to the G.H.Q neighbourhood and rehearsed with the tanks for the Cambrai offensive.

Nov 20th 1917. The battalion attacked & gained their objective. Nov 30th they were in support to the 8th & 9th R. Fusiliers when the Huns counter-attacked & though severely hammered lost little ground, that evening the three battalions were thoroughly mixed up and holding on together, relieved on the night of the 1st/2nd Dec. going N to Fleurbaix where they spent Christmas. From then until March 21st they were in and out of the line about 5 miles S of Armentieres. Relieved on March 21st and on the night of 24th/25 were pushing forward through Albert to ascertain the whereabouts of the Hun, ordered back to hold the banks of the Ancre, taking up a defensive position in Aveluy Wood.

Attacked about the 27th March holding the Hun with little loss of ground, were attacked again but eventually after April 5th when the Hun made his last effort, the line became stable.

The summer up to the the middle of July was spent in and out of the line around Bouzincourt.

In July moved to near Moreuil (S. of Amiens), behind the French to be fattened for the last 100 days.

Aug 8th occupied the line just S of Morlancourt continuing in and out attacking and supporting in those hectic days, finally going out E. of Epehy at the end of September. During this period the Battalion attacked as many as 9 times in 13 days.

Moved again to St Eloi N of Arras expecting a little easier time but were immediately asked to advance and attack again.

The Battalion finally arrived at Somain from which place the Cadre returned to Chichester.

4th Feb. 1919. Consecration and Presentation of Colours by Prince of Wales.

March 1919. Reduced to Cadre.

16th June 1919. Cadre entrain for England.

Harold.

9th Officers Cadet Battalion. Camp at Gailes, Ayrshire.

23/4/17.

Our Coy. Sergt. Instructor.

Isle of Arran from Gailes Ap. 1917.

Auchans Nr Dondonald, Ayrshire.
April/17

Auchans Nr Dondonald, Ayrshire.

Auchans.

Sgt. Coghill.

Hutmates.

Irvin Munition Works. April 1917.

On the road from Kilmarnock to Gailes.

Gazetted to the Queens Regiment (Royal West Surreys) and returned to France at the end of May 1917, by way of Sittingbourne, Kent; the training camp for the Regiment. Thence to Etaples where one spent a perspiring and hetic week at the "Bull Ring". All base camps whether in England or France seemed to be organised for the purpose of making all ranks anxious to return to the line as the lesser evil of the two. I for one certainly welcomed the orders to proceed up the line to join the 2nd Battalion at Courcelles where they were resting after the fighting at Bullecourt.

The Battalion was then commanded by Lt.Col. Longbourne D.S.O. with Capt. Stroud M.C. as their very able Adjutant.

After a few weeks spent with B. Coy one had the pleasure of getting to work with the Batt. scouts and enjoying the greater freedom of this job.

The part of the line we occupied from Bullecourt for 2 or 3 thousand yards to the north, offered more scope for sniping and observation than any previous bit of line I had known. The new rank enabled me to get into touch with the Gunners, Machine Gunners, Trench Mortars, including the enthusiastic officer in charge of the "Pig" (heaviest mortar). So we worried the Hun in a number of ways and added to his casualties. We ourselves lost none from sniping, but through carelessness on someones part a Hun sniper spotted one "post" and promptly put a bullet through the telescope and with admirable accuracy continuing to score bullseyes until the hole was plugged with sand bags, then proceeding to crawl out in front in the succession of shell holes to be better able to locate the marksman, came within the range of view of another Hun sniper. The bullet grazed the rim of the shellhole, sending a splash of earth down our necks just as we had slithered into cover. In the meantime from another of our own posts the sniper on duty had spotted this enthusiast and quietened him effectively, we also were able to at least persuade the first Hun sniper that two could play at his game, although unknowingly at the time the game had been played by four, one after the other.

Romanscamp 18.6.17.

Orchard at Courcelles shewing fruit trees cut down by the Huns before retiring.

from Bienvillers - Fonquevillers Rd. corner of Hannescamps and remnants of trees at Essars.

Canadian lumbermen working in the forests of France. Vadencourt Wood 21·7·17.

Canadian Lumbermen

Hauling Timber.

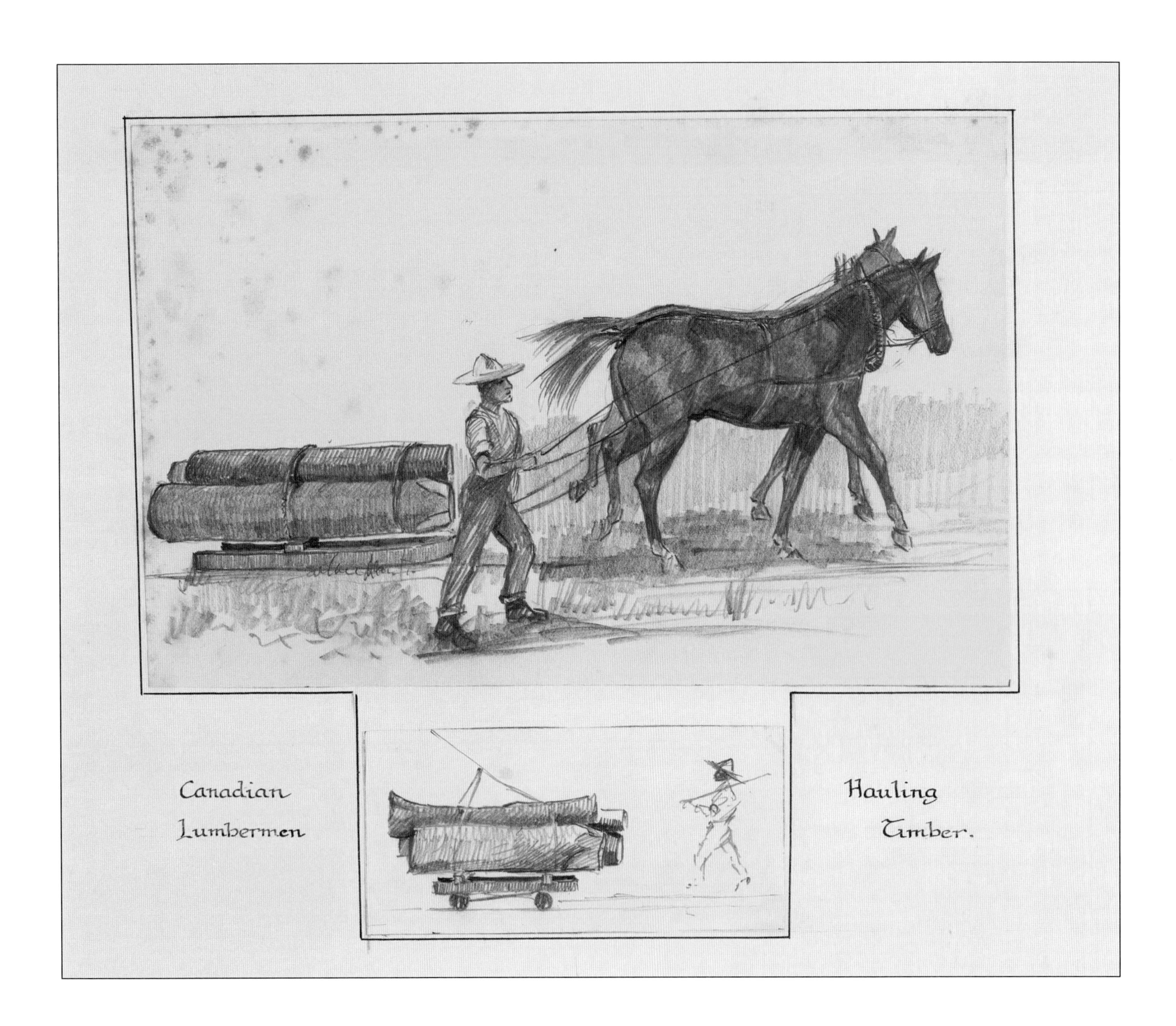

Mens Billet. St Leger 24.6.17.

Batt. H.Q. Stables at remains of Chateau. St Leger. 25.6.17.

Sketch of Hindenburg Line and Hendecourt from a point occupied by the 2nd Batt. The Queens in the Hindenburg line N.W. of Bullecourt. A Mebu is visible and one of some interest as being the spot at about which much useful sniping was carried out.
The cross in rear of Mebu is, presumably, in memory of a Bosch who died of, over exposure.

Mebus or German Strong Point. H.L. N.W. of Bullecourt. a Coy. H.Qrs 5.7.17.

Trench occupied by Germans on April 1st 17.
2nd Queens assisting in capture of Croiselles on that date.

Remains of Church

C. Trenches leading to our F. Line 6·7·17.

Croiselles from St Leger.

The Germans left few trees standing before retiring, these are by the roadside at St Leger.

Gog and Magog

Names given to two Mebu, N.W. of Bullecourt, both were used as advanced posts by the Germans. Patrols from each side sometimes meeting here during the night. The Bosch finally decided to strengthen and hold same, he was allowed to carry out the work of wiring and entrenching, also bringing a store of Grenades to the posts. Our 6" Howitzers then devoted an afternoon to effectively demolishing his past nights labours.

From the tent at camp S. of St Ledger looking S.   Ervillers & main Arras-Bapaume Rd   .   July-17.

Road near Vadencourt.

Berles-au-Bois.

Berles-au-Bois. A village but a short distance in rear of our Front Line before the German retirement of 1917. It had not been badly shelled during the whole length of time of the German occupation of this part of the line. It was to this quiet backwater we came after our occupation of the Hindenburg line at Bullecourt.

From here I and other Officers of the 7th. Division travelled by Lorry one long day right up to Ypres in advance of our Battalions, and two days later I had the distinction to become its first casualty here, the day that the Division arrived.

So at last, and I was glad that I also came to be again of that vast company, of all those old good comrades, touched by the white hot fingers of the War.

Book 1. commenced whilst on leave 1916.
Book V. finished February. 1921.

Rear cover: Memoir Vol. 5

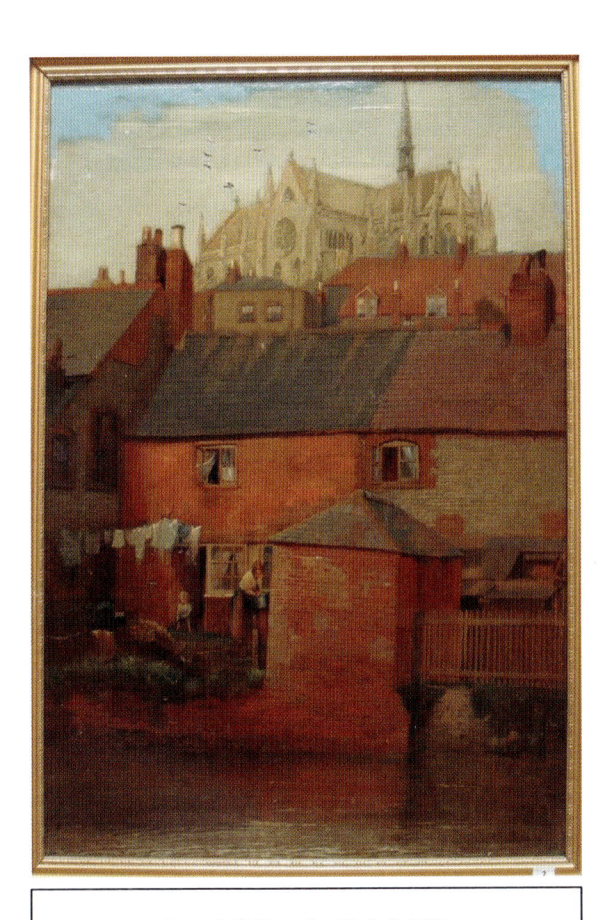

Arundel View by Ralph Ellis

THE AFTERMATH – LIFE AFTER THE WAR

Arriving at Dover on 5th September 1917 on the hospital ship *St David*, Ralph was about to embark on a long period of medical treatment. A Medical Board on the 12th September reports his injuries as a 'fracture of humerus, probably extending into elbow joint and some damage to forearm but no fracture, wounds are septic with considerable discharge.' According to his officer service record, in total he underwent six operations on his left arm over a period of two years. Much of that time was spent in various hospitals including the Lady Evelyn Mason hospital at 16 Bruton Street, London and the Prince of Wales Hospital, Marylebone, London, as well as the 2nd Eastern General in Brighton and the Military Hospital in Chichester.[120]

Nearly three years after he was wounded Ralph was still appearing in front of medical boards. The report of the Proceedings of a Medical Board on 25th June 1920, which appears from his records to be the last he attended, states that he suffered from stiffness in his elbow, partial loss of use of his left arm and hand, scarring, aching after use and wasted muscles. According to his daughter his elbow was permanently 'fixed' in an 'L' shape and the muscles in his arm and hand remained wasted all his life.[121] Having begun to compile his memoir while on leave in 1916, Ralph worked on it while in hospital and convalescing in 1917-18, and it was finally finished in 1921.

On 8th October 1918 Ralph received notification that his commission would be relinquished 'on account of ill health caused by wounds'. This decision was based on the opinion of a Medical Board dated 5th September, which said he was permanently unfit for any service. Despite the fact that he was still undergoing treatment in hospital, Ralph clearly disagreed. In a letter written on 14th October Ralph acknowledged the opinion of his last Medical Board but argued that his injuries were 'not sufficient' to stop him carrying out the duties of an infantry officer on active service, which he was willing to resume forthwith. He was called for an interview but his request was dismissed, as was his suggestion that he might be employed as a draughtsman – it being considered 'impossible to employ an officer as a draughtsman'. The relinquishment stood, confirmed in a letter dated 30th October 1918.[122]

What Ralph may or may not have known was that on the day the order to relinquish his commission was issued, October 8th, the army introduced a new instruction to 'hold up all cases [of relinquishment] where the officer was in hospital'. Correspondence in his officer service record shows that there was some doubt as to whether it was

---

[120] TNA WO 339/83413.
[121] Gowler (1997): 39.
[122] TNA WO 339/83413.

Ralph and Gertrude Ellis

intended to cancel retrospective cases like Ralph's, but as there was no definitive instruction the decision was made that his relinquishment should stand.[123]

It is difficult to ascertain Ralph's financial situation from the evidence in his officer service record. It appears that for the first year, while he was in hospital and undergoing surgery, he received wound gratuities totalling £104 3s 4d. From 30th August 1918, the anniversary of his injury, he received a wound pension of £50 a year for the next four years. This was calculated according to the severity of his disability as assessed by a Medical Board.[124] There is no evidence of any further payments. He was left in reduced circumstances with little support, a common feature of the treatment of disabled servicemen.

However, opportunities for re-training for ex-servicemen did exist. In October 1920 Ralph registered at the Slade School of Art in London, embarking on a course in Drawing, Painting and Design funded by an Ex-Service Grant, which covered his fees of £29 8s a year for two years. Studying for six days a week during term-time he gained certificates in Decorative Design, Painting from Life and Figure Drawing. A note in his Slade registry file says that he was, 'One of the men under the grant who has made the most progress, I should not be surprised if he developed into a very good painter indeed'.[125] Written by his tutor and Slade Professor of Fine Art, Henry Tonks, this was praise indeed. Tonks was known for his caustic manner and was notoriously critical of his students.[126]

When Ralph went to war Gertrude Ellis stayed in Bognor Regis, running their shop which sold home decorating and artists' materials. At some point during the war she gave up the shop and worked as a secretary to the matron at Haslar Hospital in Gosport. By July 1920 Ralph was living at 2 Grenville Street, W.C.1, where Gertrude joined him while he was studying. After the Slade the couple returned to Sussex, taking up residence in Arundel where Ralph's father and sister still lived.[127] Ralph had returned to his roots in the heart of his beloved Sussex Downs.

The next challenge was how he was to make a living as an artist. A solution emerged when Henty & Constable, the local brewers, asked him to paint signs for their public houses. He started with a few examples to show what he could do, but went on to design and paint signs for their 250 pubs and inns in Sussex, Surrey and Hampshire. He also maintained the signs and over the next three decades he built a very fruitful career. By the end of the 1920s Ralph was taking commissions from all over the country, designing and painting more than 300 signs for other breweries. In 1926 Ralph

---

[123] Ibid.
[124] Ibid.
[125] UCLCA/SR.
[126] Royal College of Surgeons, https://livesonline.rcseng.ac.uk, accessed 6 January 2019.
[127] Gowler (1997): 39; UCLCA/SR.

Ralph Ellis: The Railway Tavern pub sign

received an international commission – a sign for the Paris brasserie, 'Les Deux Magots', a meeting place for Parisian intellectual society, which was in its heyday.

The signs needed to withstand the elements and required considerable preparation both before and after painting, as well as transporting to and from the public houses, work that was carried out by a small team of local people from premises situated close to the River Arun in Arundel. Each inn's location required a different style of sign and Ralph conducted meticulous research for his images, particularly when designing a portrait, for example for the General Abercrombie or the King's Head. Lettering was another of Ralph's specialities; many of the images on his inn signs were accompanied by fine lettering and he also took commissions for sign writing on shop fronts and trade vans.[128]

Ralph's first love was landscape painting, which he resumed after the war, first as a hobby and later, as he gained confidence and became more proficient, for sale. His favourite medium was oil paint, in which he painted over two hundred pictures, in addition to around thirty-six watercolours and a few pencil drawings. The subjects were mainly Sussex scenes, in the vicinity of Arundel, that he could reach by bus as he did not drive due to his disability. He exhibited widely in the local area and his paintings were very popular, selling for sums that would be worth several hundred pounds today. Although he retired from inn-sign painting in 1951, he continued to paint landscapes right up to his death in 1963.[129]

For many years Ralph and Gertrude had wanted to start a family and in 1923 their son David was born followed in 1927 by another son who only lived for four days. Their daughter, Margaret, whose biography of her father has provided much of the information for this chapter, was born in 1928. By then the Ellis family had moved from the High Street in Arundel to 47, Maltravers Street, where Ralph was to live for the rest of his life. He worked in a studio in King's Arms Hill, which was reached from the bottom of their garden. For a few years all went well, Ralph's business increased and the children grew, but in 1932 David died of whooping chough and rheumatic fever, a terrible blow to Ralph and Gertrude. Margaret says, '… life stopped for the Ellis family once more'.[130]

With the outbreak of the Second World War Ralph once again stepped up to do his duty. As Arundel prepared for war in 1939 he was appointed Fuel Overseer, a paid post at a salary of £100 p.a. plus office expenses and clerical assistance, using the study of 47, Maltravers Street as an office. He volunteered for the Home Guard and, due to his disability, he became Quartermaster Sergeant, in charge of stores and he also became an A.R.P. Warden, cycling around his beat. Alongside these duties Ralph found

[128] Gowler (1997) 40, 41, 63.
[129] Ibid.
[130] Ibid: 76.

Downland View by Ralph Ellis

time to continue his work painting inn signs. However, it was his great love of landscape painting that suffered; he produced only a very few landscapes during the war years.[131]

Why Ralph revisited his Great War memoir in 1948 is a mystery; perhaps the second global conflict in thirty years prompted his returning to the first. For this version, which was typewritten with some amendments, he chose to focus only on the text. Entitled 'A March with the Infantry' by 428 (his Regimental number from the 7th Royal Sussex), the revised version is dedicated to the infantry battalions and the men who served in them during the Great War.

After the Second World War life settled down with Ralph returning to his inn sign work and resuming his landscape painting. The Ellis family was an important part of the Arundel community, involved in the life of St Nicholas Church and also taking part in amateur dramatics, with Ralph participating as an actor, a stage manager and a scenery painter. They had many friends and enjoyed social gatherings and parties. Although the family was never well off, they enjoyed the simple things in life, particularly walking in the local countryside, and had a few holidays exploring other parts of the United Kingdom.[132]

When he retired in 1951 Ralph continued to paint and to enjoy the countryside around Arundel, which he loved. Gertrude died in 1960, which was very distressing for Ralph as they had been together for fifty years and had shared the sadness of losing two hildren. Gertrude was always a great support to Ralph, helping him with his business and in the aftermath of the war. Three years later, in May 1963, Ralph was taken ill and died. He was 78 years old and had lived for 45 years after the end of the First World War.[133]

In a sense Ralph was one of the lucky ones. He returned from the war and despite his injuries, which left him permanently disabled, pieced his life back together and made a success of it. This was not always the case; thirty-three thousand officers were left with some kind of physical or mental disability ranging from severe to slight, and many struggled to return to normality. The severe cases were institutionalised and the less damaged were largely left to get on with it. However, many of them did what Ralph did and put the experience behind them. The question is why he was able to do that.

Perhaps most importantly, Ralph had a wife to return to. Gertrude was there to support him through his initial lengthy recovery from his wounds and later through the periods of depression that he suffered throughout his life. It is impossible to be certain if these dark periods were a legacy of the war, but his daughter recalls them and

---

[131] Ibid: 84-85.
[132] Ibid: 110-116.
[133] Gowler (1997): 127, 135-6.

Ralph Ellis at his easel

also quotes from one of his notebooks, 'I am groping my way through a black night and my soul is like the wind howling through the sapless branches of a forest of dead trees.'[134] But it seems that these periods were rare and most of the time Ralph enjoyed life, his work, his painting, his children and living in the quiet and beautiful town of Arundel surrounded by the glorious Sussex countryside.

Ralph's decision to become an artist would have been more difficult had the injury been to his right arm. As it was he was able to function well with the use of just his right arm, enjoying swimming and cycling and, of course, painting. So he was able to pursue a successful career doing something he loved in beautiful surroundings. His career also gave him the chance to travel and he undertook trips, both for business and pleasure, in the British Isles, Ireland and even back to France.[135]

Perhaps the act of writing his memoir after the Great War was in some way cathartic. Revisiting his experiences and placing them in some kind of narrative enabled him to move on. Although the physical scars remained with him, this may have helped to mitigate the mental trauma, although nonetheless he was prone to periods of depression. Despite all he had been through, Ralph survived and led a significant life.

In 1995 West Sussex County Council erected a blue plaque to Ralph's memory on 47, Maltravers Street, the house he had lived in for thirty-six years. It commemorates his career as an 'Artist, Painter and Designer of Inn Signs'. He will also be remembered for his account of his experiences in the 7th Battalion, Royal Sussex Regiment during the Great War. Whatever the reason for writing his memoir, it left behind a lasting memorial to the Sussex men who marched with the infantry.

---

[134] Ibid: 79.
[135] Ibid: 35, 75, 79.

IN
THIS HOUSE
LIVED

RALPH ELLIS
1885 - 1963

ARTIST
PAINTER & DESIGNER
OF
INN SIGNS

WEST SUSSEX COUNTY COUNCIL

APPENDIX: LETTERS FROM THE FRONT

Introduction

While serving with the 7th Battalion, Royal Sussex Regiment, Ralph wrote home frequently to his family. Some of his letters to his parents and sisters survived the war and in 1956 he selected extracts from the letters, retaining twenty-five of them in typewritten form. These extracts are reproduced in their entirety below. Ralph also wrote to his wife, Gertrude, but the letters have not survived.[136]

Ralph's letters from France and Belgium are significant for several reasons. For the recipients they were a tangible link to Ralph. They did not know if or when they would see him again and for this reason alone the family treasured them. They were also important to Ralph, as he took the trouble to edit and type them some 40 years after the war. Along with the notes and sketches he made while serving, he used some material from the letters in his memoir.

From a historical perspective letters are valuable primary sources. Often Ralph's letters were written within hours or at most a few days of events occurring, providing an insight into his experiences and mindset, which was less likely to be affected by the unreliability of memory. Because the letters are dated it is possible to read them alongside the Battalion War Diary, complimenting the official record with Ralph's personal experiences.

All letters written by soldiers in the ranks were subject to censorship, which was exercised by the junior officers. An example of this can be seen in Ralph's letter to Edith dated September 19th, 1916. Without mentioning where the Battalion was and what they were doing, Ralph told his family about his life in the army. While he described life in the trenches, the wiring parties in no man's land and being under shell fire, he also talked about the weather, the food, the state of the trenches, the lack of sleep, his health, his experiences as an observer working with the artillery. Once out of the trenches, with more time to write, he described life behind the lines, the farmhouses where they were billeted, the local French and Belgian people, the ruined villages, and the joys of nature. He was careful not to alarm them, often relating amusing anecdotes and downplaying the horrors and hardships he was experiencing. He took great pains to reassure them that despite the circumstances, he was in good health and standing up well to army life.

Why Ralph selected these particular letters is unknown; perhaps they were the most interesting, or the most representative or just the ones that survived. Margaret Gowler

---

[136] WSRO, RSR Archive, AM1242; Gowler (1997)

notes an unexplained gap in the correspondence of six months between March 28th and September 12th 1916. She suggests that the most likely reason is that letters were written but were either mislaid or deliberately not retained. Ralph's track record as a conscientious correspondent makes it unlikely that he would have simply stopped writing during this period. However, the missing six months coincided with the Battalion training for and participating in the Battle of the Somme. During busy periods the men sent Field Post Cards, which were pre-printed with basic information to be deleted as appropriate, to enable them to keep their families informed of their wellbeing. Ralph refers to having sent a succession of these in September 1916.

The Army was well aware of the importance of the postal service in maintaining morale among the troops. According to the official history of the Royal Mail, 'Not far short of 5 million parcels went to France in the month before Christmas, 1916. Supplies of tobacco and cigarettes… remained a staple item at all times of the year… Outbound letters peaked at more than 12 million a week early in the first quarter of 1918.'[137] Letters travelling in either direction would only take a day or two to reach their destination. However, when the post failed to materialize, the men showed 'considerable displeasure' as this was 'the event of the day'.[138]

The letters illustrate the importance of contact with family and friends at home for those serving overseas. As well as the frequent correspondence going backwards and forwards, Ralph's family sent many parcels, for which he was very grateful. Items such as socks, warm clothing and magazines as well as necessities like soap and shaving equipment were popular, as were food treats to supplement the mundane army diet. As important as receiving parcels was hearing about life at home. Ralph was keen to learn what they were reading in the newspapers as people at home often know more about the progress of the war than those involved, and how they were faring with bread rationing. This link with normal life and home was vital for men enduring events and conditions so far removed from their past experience.

---

[137] Campbell-Smith (2011): 222-4, quoted in Godfrey [n.d.]; Appendix, p. 273.
[138] Letter dated 10 November 1916.

Letters

18.6.1915

My dear Mother,

We are enjoying a quiet time now, which gives us all an opportunity of a good clean up.

I think I told you about the affectionate cow, have also discovered that it has a remarkable appetite, it quite enjoys soapy water and hard biscuits. Yesterday, I found it on the point of chewing a pair of my socks which I had just washed and left for a moment.

I had my biggest laugh just before, the Company Q.M.S. and Company Sergeant Major had arranged a nice little meal under the shade of some trees. The meal included half a long French loaf, I think the cow had already observed the attractive morsel and made off with it as soon as their backs were turned. The Q.M.S gave a truly British yell and charged after it, it was very funny to see that animal bolting off with half a loaf in its mouth, it did not carry it very far and Q.M.S. spent the succeeding ten minutes in a lurid description of the poor old cow, finally giving what was left of the loaf to a nearby horse out of spite.

26.6.1915

Dear Edith,

So you would like a little more blood and thunder in my letters, well, fortunately we have not seen much. Apparently one of our fellows did his best to make up for the deficiency in one of his letters home. It was told to us by an Officer during the course of a lecture on writing and the censoring of same. This man was writing of his first experience in the trenches and wrote 'How they had a very warm time of it,' we did so far as the weather was concerned, and went on to describe how they jumped on to the parapet, charging the Germans who ran before them, hands in the air, screaming with pain.

Well, it was not anything like that. We shall shortly have a further experience of the trenches and will try to give you a better description.

My first experience of being under fire was not in the trenches at all. We were in support well behind the firing line. Orders were given that a certain number of men were to go to dig a communication trench. I thought it a good opportunity to test my range finder at night on the star shells that so continually uncover the darkness, so went with the party.

After a short march by road, then by devious ways through fields by ruined farm dwellings and buildings, but land which is still cultivated and with cattle grazing, and seldom appear to be hit by a stray bullet or shell; we came to the allotted place and digging began. Our first line trench was not far away, neither were the Germans, but rifle fire was not at all heavy, but quite a possible chance of being seen when the star shells were bursting. It appeared to me much like a day or night at the rifle ranges, only at the wrong end, with a Brock's Benefit thrown in. We had but one casualty. I heard what sounded like a hare's scream, hit by a stray bullet. Before daylight appeared we had to be on our way again.

My range finding was not a success.

28.6.1915

Dear Mother,

Very many thanks for the parcel. I have carved my way into the cake, it will soon be a memory only.

You should see my small dug-out, it is nicely boarded inside and so can be kept quite clean. I am going to call it 'Frog-Halt' for the reason that frogs of all sizes inhabit the trenches here, and some of the dug-outs, they come to a full stop at mine, as they cannot manage the high jump into it.

We are fairly comfortable and quiet here, with plenty of work to do and I am really enjoying myself more than in the billets.

We work all night and obtain our sleep during the day. As it is our first day in these trenches, I have been busy taking our various ranges and making myself as useful as possible, with the pencil. I have not seen a German soldier yet, although I have had splendid views of part of their lines and the crumpled up houses and farms beyond. A good deal of sniping is carried out on either side but I think our chaps are quite a match for the Germans.

10.7.15

Dear Edith

Thanks for your letter, I intended writing to you before and will try to make amends now.

We are in the trenches now so there is so little time for it. A good deal of work to be done at night, hard work too, some of it, digging new dug-outs, re-building parapets, etc. Then of course there is food to be cooked, so that one likes to get down to sleep when there is time to spare.

Our quietest period is from dawn to about 3pm, it is strange fighting, living here in a semi-private fashion. Occasionally there is a burst of shelling, we hear the shells shriek over our heads and if you have sufficient energy, jump up to see where they burst, bullets occasionally whiz over or strike close at hand, that is warfare as at present fought, but I guess things will hum a little more before long.

We have a very pretty cat here with us, also a dog, both are good chums and seem to enjoy trench life, probably because they are so well fed. "Harold" our own regimental mascot and pet stays at headquarters along with the other celebrities.

We found it very stormy coming into the trenches this time, lightning very vivid with heavy rain, making the trenches very bad for moving about in, we slipped and slid along the whole way. In one section the trench runs right through a long row of houses, here it was pitch dark and we held on to each other's pack or equipment as the only means of maintaining connection. Quite impossible to see one another. A light would have attracted heavy fire immediately.

Yesterday I was out scouting for material to add to the comfort of my dug-out and came upon the house of a decorator. A row of houses much battered about, a quick bolt across the road and into the decorator's shop. The front room instantly made me think of Jack, the wall had been divided into panels on which were paintings of deer and landscapes, not badly done either. At the back was the paint shop and what a scene! Dry colours, stencils, glass and all the other paraphernalia of a painter's shop just shot about all over the place. The painter's last job was there too. A painted drain-pipe, partly decorated to be intended, no doubt, for an umbrella stand. Upstairs were a few pictures, china and remains of clothing littered about. The roof down in one place and the walls pierced in places for offensive purposes. A little too hot for them, I think, for many bullets had struck through the not very thick walls.

I took away with me a blind, to shelter my dug-out from rain and sun whilst I slept during the day, two of the pictures ornament the walls of the trench.

12.7.1915

My dear Mother,

Thanks ever so much for the parcel which arrived just after we came out of trenches and I was feeling I should like something good.

We have plenty of food in the trenches, but the day's rations are issued in one batch, and it is quite a job to keep it clean or anything like it on hot days. The trenches swarm with flies, nasty blue ones. Up to the present, that has been my worst annoyance. One other thing, I dislike very much too. I think I have told you that during the night, we must crawl out in front of the trench to repair the wire entanglements or the parapet. That's quite all right, the rotton part of the business is when the German sentries fire a star shell to light up "No Man's Land". Down we must lay flat at once. What you actually lay on is bad enough with all the litter from the trenches. Once I felt something warm, in one hand, for a fraction of a second I thought it must be the hand of a "Jerry" I was going to clutch, then a mouse ran out from between finger and thumb. Worse still, on another occasion, my nose entered the smelly half emptied tin of bully beef, and a hoard of blow flies flew about my face in great alarm.

What I am laying on is I think the worst of all, and squirm inwardly the whole time and would rather risk standing up, but that might make it bad for others, no doubt I shall get used to it. N.B. I did not and remained standing in future.

We all had a hot bath yesterday and a change of underclothing. This is worth recording. I enjoyed it so thoroughly. Have just had a nice clean shave at a barber's close by, by just a bit of a girl, a Belgian refugee, no talking, as with an English barber, but a good shave. Womanlike, she must needs stop to look out of the window several times.

21.7.1915

My dear Edith,

I write to you fairly frequently, but each time there is a good parcel of luxuries to thank you for and they are so expensive to buy and send out. However, you have the satisfaction of knowing how greatly they are appreciated. "Punch" was a great treat.

Tobacco is issued each week and sometimes a quantity is supplied from a private source. Yesterday, I issued to my section, seven packets of cigarettes per man. Not bad, eh?

The Oxo cubes assist my efforts at cooking stew, much more appetizing.

I think we shall be up in the front line trenches again tonight. We are not out of range here, even of rifle fire and the other morning we had quite a shower of shells drop close to us.

Yesterday, I was in charge of a guard close by and during the day a few shells came over, falling about 200 yards further up the road. The first I knew of it was to see three oldish men come scuttling down the road as hard as they could go and make a dive for our dug-out, next came a boy and then a woman from a house nearby. They filled the dug-out. After all was peaceful again, they departed, calling out as they went, "Fin-ish. Fin-ish" and so back to their work again. It is terrible for the civilians who hang on to their homes, carrying on just as before the war, they suffer for it. I was looking at a field yesterday, where peasants were busy carrying the hay and the country lovely and peaceful, yet only the previous day, just before we cooked our breakfast, six shrapnel shells burst over that same field. One can get used to it but I'm thinking that English haymakers would look for double pay to work those fields.

2.8.1915

My dear Emma,

No doubt you will remember that tall lad by the name of Short, he is in the same Platoon as myself. I have an interesting job just now, in charge of guard at the point where all civilians are forbidden to go further, unless they can produce a pass. Those who have one, smile and look rather superior, and those without a pass, jabber away trying to make all kinds of explanations no doubt, but they have to go back.

It is Sunday and I am able to watch the French and Belgian people go by to Mass. Some of the ladies look very nice and smart in their Sunday best, very few wear hats, a sensible idea in this warm weather.

I think I told you that our last period in the front line trench was quite close to the German front line, not more than 70 yards in some places. A case of keeping your head well down during the day and serious for those who forgot, apart from that, it was quiet. I had one exciting half hour, going one night to find if the wire in front was in good shape. It was weak in one place, and the following night provided suitable weather for the job, very dark and pouring with rain. One officer came and two privates to help with the ready-made wood and wire entanglement. They are very awkward to handle, more so than a five barred gate, though not so heavy. I have had more pleasant jobs than getting that over the parapet and into position without making a noise; almost an impossibility owing to the numerous tins scattered about in front of the trench. We fixed it, but I think I must have made a noise on putting up some old barbed wire to complete the job. German sentries started firing, being so close the flash from the rifles could be easily seen, we laid flat and the shots went over us. As they kept up the fire, we made our way back flat on our stomachs, through soaking wet tangles of weeds, soft clay and broken tins, the debris from the trenches and the rain pouring down all the time. Very pretty we looked too when we got back. It was much more exciting than anything previously experienced.

One thing we can obtain here not far from the firing line is a good swim in clean water. I much appreciate it and look forward to one when I come off guard duty.

Today we peeled our potatoes in France, then took them to be cooked in Belgium but we shall eat them in France. Hope to add some runner beans to the meal. Fresh vegetables are a great luxury.

9.8.1915

My dear Mother,

Just a few lines, as I know you are anxious to hear from me.

The last period was rather trying, working out in front at night can be quite exciting and exhilarating, after a time it becomes trying. We had already experienced one of our mines or saps going up, blowing a part of the German trench to pieces. This time while on trench duty about 4 a.m. I heard an awful rumbling and the trench I was in, swayed a bit, for the moment it was not easy to grasp what was happening, but seeing earth and stones flying high in the air, the rumbling noise too grew louder, making me realize what was "up" immediately we poured in a rapid rifle fire, the Mine was a failure, I think it damaged their own trench pretty badly.

Yesterday (Sunday) we were under shell fire, but this morning we are now in support, beat everything, we were awakened just before 4 a.m. and realized at once that we were under very heavy shell fire. It lasted about 2 hours or more.

It is impossible to describe it, they shrieked over in coveys, one continuous stream and mostly high explosives. During one brief interval, I heard the sound of a cock crowing in the distance, such a vivid contrast, like someone opening a window, it is wonderful how one can get used to even such experience. For the first ten minutes, what with waking suddenly, the cold and the nerves, I shook from head to foot, in spite of all my efforts to control myself.

As time wore on, I found myself dozing, having so shortly left the front line, we were all so very tired and waking every now and then as a shell fell close by and shaking the ground by the explosion. I was very conscious that our shelter had but a foot of earth on the roof.

We were not sorry when the activity ceased. By the greatest good fortune, the trench we occupied was not actually struck.

It was quite miraculous and I felt thankful. After a walk down to H.Q. I am really going to get a little sleep.

By the way, are quinine pills useful for putting the stomach right?

I am not ill, but occasionally it refuses food, sort of goes on strike, for which I sometimes cannot blame it.

12.8.1915

Dear Edith,

I was delighted to hear from you and to receive parcel etc. We do our own cooking in this particular trench under difficult conditions and in a very confined space, consequently by the time the water is boiled and the bacon cooked, we are smoked out and have shed enough tears to pickle the bacon in. There are two other Sergeants in this dug-out for dinner today, so we regaled ourselves with the salmon you sent, and so had no bother with cooking.

We have not been treated to any more bombardments which I wrote of to Mother. I understand that about 2,000 shells were put over our bit of the front in that 2 hours or so.

Whilst we were in the front line last week, I was startled to hear a sudden burst of rifle fire from our trench to the right, and running out of my dug-out found it was brought about by a small number of wild duck flying parallel and a little to the rear of our trench. Everyman along the lines was letting drive at them with his rifle, forgetting or not caring that all these bullets were sailing back behind our lines. One duck was brought down and away went a man after it, naturally the Germans over the way, distance no further than from home to Bridge House, had also been watching and noted where it fell, in rough ground in full view from the German trench.

Our fellow did a proper crawl towards it, but the German snipers were no sportsmen and Cheeseman had to retire hastily. We left the trench the same day and learned that the relief secured the duck during darkness.

We are in support here and I am just going back behind our lines for a swim this afternoon, a great luxury, although I never expected to be able to indulge in such things out here within 2,000 yards of the German front line.

Later an officer of "C" Coy. Enjoying a swim, got a little out of his course and was shot in the behind, most unfortunate, as the nurses chafed him a great deal for having his back to the enemy.

22.8.1915

My dear Mother,

Many thanks for letters from both you and Dad. It is good of you all to write so frequently, naturally we out here find the arrival of the post, the most interesting event of the day.

It is a lovely August day, Arundel and the Downs must be looking wonderful when I think of all that, I feel happy that there, all the homes are intact, not torn to pieces or burnt as we unfortunately are so used to seeing them here.

Thank you for your offer of papers, we have a few issued to us now and again, and whilst in billets, are able to buy any we please, they cost 2d each.

The paper man or woman blows a horn, like old Dearling, the carrier from Amberley to Arundel did, to warn us of his approach.

So young Butcher from Barnet is making range finders, no doubt you informed him that I was using one!

I think the manipulation must be much more interesting than assisting in the construction of the instrument.

The day we came out of the trenches, I was looking through mine from an observation post right up in the roof of a damaged house, the two eyes of the instrument looking through gaps in the tiles, whilst I was well concealed.

Such a splendid view I had overlooking the level countryside. A few shells were bursting up on our right, I saw too, a mine blow up, a great volume of black smoke shot up into the air, to be followed by the sound of the explosion. I was there to try and obtain a range of the roads, but patiently watching, I could see figures passing along in certain directions, in fact, a good deal of traffic, but difficult to distinguish which were civilians and which were troops.

All most interesting and wonderful too that as these figures passed along that distant road, so my instrument recorded their distance from me, providing I did my part thoroughly and accurately, I was also able to spot new workings, the earth could be detected thrown up in shovel fulls, although happening more than a mile away.

My work is to attempt to draw that small section, add the various ranges and any remarks on what I had seen that might be even remotely useful.

Many thanks for the pills, they certainly seem to have done me good, but you must not think that I am unwell. You would not think so if you could see me.

28.8.1915

My dear Mother,

We are enjoying splendid weather, cloudless days and moonlit nights. I hope that it will continue. It has been so light that we can see clearly the German trenches at night, but the mornings are cold and the nights grow longer. In the trenches we work up to about 1 a.m. and unless on sentry duty remain in the trench and sleep if we can.

A walk along the trench in the early hours reminds me of a walk I once took along the Thames embankment in the early hours and seeing figures huddled up and sleeping in any available corner, in all manner of positions.

In the trenches opposite, we have a very quiet lot. They have been waving their hands to fellows and exposing themselves quite plainly, in fact we have seen more Germans this morning than during all the time we have been in the line. Should say that this lot were much more anxious for peace than to try to carve their way to Calais or Paris.

We hear a good deal of heavy gun fire going on somewhere which does not sound at all like Peace.

A large catapult, of all things has been erected, just outside my dugout, not at all welcome. This is for throwing grenades across the 100 yards of "No Man's Land". We tried it with a few tins of corned beef which must have pleased the Germans, but he was a brave man who picked up the first tin. The first grenades were apt to miss fire and everyone fled for their lives, including myself.

I am told a German "Taube" was shot down yesterday, at the time I was peacefully sleeping, it requires a great deal of excitement to persuade one to rouse up and neglect the opportunity to sleep, so did not see it come down.

22.9.1915

My dear Mother,

We continue to enjoy splendid weather, although rather cold at night. Dad must have found it very warm walking to Poling, apart from the warmth, I'm sure he must have enjoyed it.

Today I have been wandering about on the ground between the front line and support trenches obtaining a few ranges that were required.

In one place, I heard a Pheasant, visions of a glorious feed rose in my mind. I was able to approach near it, but not a chance of a shot, far too much cover just there and I heard no more of it, but it was the means of my enjoying a little feast of blackberries and obtaining some green stuff from a long neglected cottage garden. I could not wait to cook it properly, but thoroughly enjoyed it.

The wild life is just like we see at home. A pair of Kestrels were hovering over the fields and a fine cock Yellow Hammer hopping about, the Tortoiseshell Butterfly is just as common here, as well as Red Admiral and Peacock and I've seen one or two good specimens of the Painted Lady. The Moorhen has the free run of the river which is rather exposed, or some of the Moorhens might have made a change of diet before now, the only other birds that I have noticed are the Heron and the Snipe.

Cecil, my understudy, came with me to take some ranges from an Observation Post. He was able to see a party of Germans marching behind their lines, it is quite an incident to be able to view the quarry.

For the last two days, we have heard incessant Artillery fire, some distance away and have wondered what my nerves would be like under a clear experience of that. However, one appears to be able to get used to most things, more or less.

21.11.1915

My dear Mother,

I thought that for a few days, I should find plenty of time for writing letters, but on Sunday whilst on guard duty, another N.C.O was sent to relieve me with orders that I must report with one other Sergt. and an Officer to Brigade H.Q at once. We were whisked off to another part of the line which was some distance away, we went by motor truck and attached to the 2nd Battn Grenadier Guards, 1st Guards Brigade, who were at the time in the firing line. We joined them there, the same night and shall remain with them, I think until the end of the week. In the meantime, our Battn will be enjoying a rest, rotten luck. I have no duties and may spend my time trying to keep warm and watch points.

I thought I knew all I require about trenches, but different units vary slightly in their methods of carrying on. The Guards naturally do the thing about right, and pay great attention to being as spick and span as possible in or out of the trenches.

A notable man is also attached to this Battalion. N.B. Winston Churchill.

He has passed through my trench once or twice, following in the wake of the C.O. and always talking, whilst the C.O is looking left and right to see all is as it should be.

No.1 Company, the Kings Co. enjoy the very doubtful privilege while in the trenches, of parading in full kit, ready to march at Reveille and Retreat. We have had some sharp night frosts, very cold standing about.

Will you please thank Edith for her very kind offer of boots and coat. As to the former, we are now being issued with long rubber boots reaching to the thigh almost, whenever we go into the line. A short warm waterproof would be very welcome, our greatcoats are long and of thick material, which in bad weather become saturated and covered with mud, especially the lower part. I could not carry both and should be "For It" if I disposed of the greatcoat.

Tomorrow night, we go up to the trenches again for another 48 hours, in the "Sussex" I think the trenches would need to be much worse than the one we occupy to warrant a 48 hour in and out spell.

Whilst in the front line a shell burst quite close to myself and two Guardsmen, destroying one of our shelters, no dug-outs, which have a roof consisting mainly of bricks and brick rubble. One of the men, a Guards Sgt. got some of the blast peppering his face with very small fragments of brick. Not much fun, I thought in having all those picked out. He thought little of it and wished to stay in the line.

4.12.1915

My dear Edith,

Many thanks for your generous offer and very tempting to accept. However, I have just discovered that we shall most probably be served out with big mackintosh cloaks, which will I trust effectively protect us from the rain.

I see that men of other Battalions already have them. I very much appreciate your good offer, Edith, it is just like you to do so.

We have just finished a rather dreary march to fresh billets, a little nearer the line. Our way took us over the low ground that stretches so far in this part of the country, roads were bad and thick with mud. In passing other troops or transport, we were forced to the side of the road which was even worse and very rough. A fine rain fell all the time, enveloping us like a vaporous fog.

I can enjoy such weather walking on high ground, but on the flats, loaded with equipment, it is depressing, and I should have liked to be away from it all and into clean clothes, a nice meal, the curtains drawn and forget the weather.

Our billet is an old barn which shelters the whole platoon, but the barn doors are missing, the wind is rising which I can hear whistling round the building and through the gap where the doors should be, making our candles flicker and gutter and sometimes go out. One more letter to write and I shall curl up with my blanket round me and so to sleep.

8.12.1915

My dear Mother,

Many thanks for your letter, so you are also having rough weather. Here, it has been very windy and a great deal of rain with it, in fact it seems to rain every day, with a few bright intervals. Very glad that we are to go back to the trenches for 48 hours in and 48 hours out. That I think will be quite long enough in this weather. It looks as though we shall be in the line for Christmas. I don't mind where we are going as long as we are in France.

We are in a very out of the way place, flat country which holds the water like a basin, the canal looks to be at a higher level than the land. Billets here vary quite a lot, mostly attached to small farms. The civilians here are not very friendly, other troops may have upset them. To make matters worse, all these small farmhouses, instead of having a nice flower garden in front of the house, choose instead to have an evil-smelling midden close to their doorstep, around which the small barns and stalls are clustered. Sometimes just as we are sitting down to a meal, the old boy will come out and stir up the midden, the result is worse than a gas attack!

I visited another billet the other evening at the far end of the village and a rather larger farm. This is worth recording, I was told that as soon as our men arrived, the people living in the big farmhouse recognized the Royal Sussex Badge and called it a "Bon regiment" and gave the men a great welcome.

Men of the 2nd and 5th Battalions of the Royal Sussex had previously been billeted at the farm. Our men were invited into the house whenever duties permitted. Every evening, they fill up both of their living rooms and make good use of the piano. I heard more Sussex songs that evening than I've ever heard before and came away thinking how fortunate that Company was in having such a good billet, glad too that the 2nd and 5th had left with such a good reputation.

Well I must give up now, too beastly cold to write for long.

10.2.1916

Just a few lines before we go up to the trenches again, tomorrow or the following day. It seems quite a time since we were in the line, not that I am particularly anxious to see them again.

With good fortune, I should soon be home on leave. I had hoped I might get away while we were out of the line for this long rest. Only one more Sergeant to go before my turn. He is away on a "Course" and if not back before the next lot depart, I shall take his place. It is not an event I dare to be too expectant about especially in the front line.

The days are lengthening a little now, we shall notice this more when back in the line. "Stand to" at dawn and evening depends of course, entirely on the time of daybreak and when the evening shadow falls. It has turned colder but fine the last day or two, but I have noticed a few spring like touches here and there.

I took my scouts out for a double along the quiet roads this morning. In passing an orchard, saw what I thought were a flock of fieldfares busily feeding on the soft spread.

This week we had a ceremonial parade at which the G.O.C. 12th Division presented the D.C.M. to one of our Sergeants. This was won some time back. I hear that other men of our Battalion are to receive decorations.

28.3.1916

My dear Mother,

Many thanks for all your letters and would like to thank Edith for hers also.

We have been up to the trenches for ten days, the last four in the front line, the support trenches were bad enough, but the last four days the worst I have experienced. The weather turned very cold, snowed heavily one night, froze the next and poured with rain the following, quite enough to put up with without enemy action.

You will see by the papers that we have lost a few while I was on leave, but some papers made the mistake of reporting that Irish troops bore it all.

I read that they now have trenches in London. We laughed at the description of the nice little dug-outs complete with table and wash basin, it might possibly describe certain trenches out here, way back. It quite fails to give any idea of trenches we occupy in this part of the line.

The wind is very cold today and blows through the old houses, not old but smashed about by shell fire, windows broken, tiles missing from the roof, however, much better than the trenches to live in. How one glories in the first night's sleep between warm blankets.

The French people are very eager to return to what is left of their homes, if some ever left them. I notice more people at this place than when we were last here, yet it was shelled again this morning and we suffered a few casualties. The houses that some live in are patched up somehow, but so cold and bare looking, living in one or two rooms furnished with scraps of furniture. The remainder of the house given over to twenty soldiers who arrive straight from the trenches, covered in mud and smelling of the earth.

The French busy themselves with their gardens, which are dug and planted and give a neat and tidier appearance to the village. How they must long for the old peace conditions? They too have relations fighting with the French army and no doubt suffering those other dangers and discomforts.

Very glad to hear that Cecil is recovering. Balchin reported sick on coming out of the line. Not wounded, but the same complaint as before. I don't know what it is, it has affected others whom I have seen. The whole body including the face, puffed up so that, at first glance, one does not recognize the man.

Note from Margaret Gowler: (Now comes a gap of six months, I don't know whether these letters are missing or whether he didn't write them, but I expect the former.)

12.9.1916

My dear Mother,

You have not heard from me for some days, probably it has seemed longer to me than to you, at least I hope so, and that consequently you have not felt anxious at all. I sent off as many Field Post Cards as possible, but under the circumstances it is difficult to get them away. Very good to receive parcels from you and Emma this morning. I did appreciate a good feed after grubbing about in dirt and discomfort for the last nine days. Some of the days were wet, which much increased the discomfort.

The shelling was heavy and continued night and day, which does not give one much mental peace.

I am not going to try and describe it all. War increases in frightfulness, there is nothing to commend it. I don't think anyone who is in the thick of it, can have a much better opinion of it than that. If it is possible for man to make such an unspeakable hell of things, it is quite time we faced about and at least tried to put as much effort into making life the very opposite to this.

I hope the reaction will send us far the other way. The need seems to be for a really great man, greatly inspired to lead us up out of these animal hates in spite of ourselves. I think the general run of mankind of any nationality are alright, or much about the same in their knowledge of good and evil. The great leader is needed. I suppose this is asking far too much, we must rely more upon each individual effort in that direction.

I am gradually being roasted alive today, it is quite cold outside, but one of our fellows has lit a coke fire, which is a trifle too much for this bivouac. All extremes here, yesterday it was bare army rations, today two parcels. I will finish up on that note, for I am sure I have not thanked you nearly enough for the cake especially. I have enjoyed all you sent me so much.

19.9.1916

My dear Edith,

What do you think of the War News now? We have heard many and various rumours lately, but know less than you do since what newspapers we can obtain, are usually two days old before we receive them. The "armoured cars" [probably tanks] are one up on us and not a copy of a German idea. The Germans are having a terribly rough time of it on the Somme, and not exactly a picnic for us!!

It seems we must put up with another winter here. Having a touch of it today, it is this cold wet weather which creates the physical discomforts. Billets are bad enough with their many difficulties, leakages, etc. the trenches are naturally far worse to put up with. I wonder what they are like, what is left of them, around Martinpunch

[Martinpuich?] to have and to hold? Well, I do not need to wonder a great deal. Emma tells me you have invited Sgt. Mullet over to Arundel. Very kind of mother and I hope that he will accept, such a fine chap and one of the first 100,000 which should be a sufficient recommendation.

Tomorrow I return for a short while into civilization again. I have been almost … [censored] in this deserted village, the time however, has passed quickly.

17.10.1916

My dear Edith

I know that succession of Field Post Cards must be quite enough to tell you that I am too busy to write, or, which is more probably, that I have not the convenience or the inclination. I hesitate to use that word, but in this case, it has a rather special meaning, which you will no doubt understand.

Your parcel arrived almost safely, but one precious sock escaped, and I was so looking forward to a good clean pair. I have used up all my little store except for the two pairs I am now wearing. Two pairs make all the difference on long marches and in the trenches.

Harry Jacobs was very fortunate to be home again so soon. Why he has been out here only five minutes while I am floating around France, it seems for years.

Please do not think me ungrateful for my present good health and strength. There are occasions when it seems scarcely possible to come through it with a whole skin, so how can one feel but very thankful.

The next great wonder to me is that for all the roughness of this life, sleeping on wet ground, getting wet through and drying off without a change of clothing, things which in peace time we should have considered meant certain illness, yet I have not had a cold or a twinge of neuralgia since I have been out here.

23.10.1916

Dear Mother and Dad,

I owe you quite a few letters, but for the last few days, it has been impossible to get letters away. I hope you have not been worried. I am quite as usual, fit and well, although some of the days, of late, have been very tough.

Weather wet and cold, followed by colder and quite sharp frosts. We are now in a little healthier spot for a short time, but the front line trenches will soon be seeing us again. Quiet ones, I hope and something resembling a trench, not a gully or a ditch half drained of water.

What weird things, the "Tanks" are, I have not seen them in action, but coming out, nosing their way down into the big shell holes and up out again. They appear from a short distance away, to glide along and resemble a whale or some prehistoric monster. The first Bosch to see such things gliding towards them must have suffered from "Cold Feet". If the war goes on much longer we are wondering what next will be used.

I hope to write a little more frequently now.

30.10.1916

My dear Mother and Dad,

The weather is now wet and windy, fortunately our billets are dry, so that it does not affect us very much.

You must not think that we are always having a rough time of it. It is Sunday evening and although not being spent in the way I should like best, we have our comforts. Our billet, an old disused cottage with a large open grate in which we have a big fire burning, our fuel, logs of wood.

The room is quite warm, and in fact, a really comfortable billet. We each have a wire bed to sleep on, which is most comfortable and of course, raises one above the damp floor. They are made of rabbit wire stretched over a rough framework of wood. With our ground sheet over the wire and blanket over the top of us, pack or boots for a pillow, we sleep as sweetly as the King himself in Buckingham Palace.

Many barns are now fitted up in this way, sometimes two or three tiers high, thus accommodating a much great number of men. In these days of wet and cold, the chief luxury is a fire. I am sorry for you at home, forced to buy all your fuel. We have an issue of coke in the trenches. In the reserve billets, the partly demolished houses have to suffer and provide fuel for us.

I have in mind, a certain village which reminds me of a timber yard in which all the timber had been spilt and torn in pieces. All the houses had been or were being demolished by shell fire. Mud and plaster walls had vanished, nothing remained but torn and splintered wood covering the whole of the village.

Sufficient timber to last the troops in that area all through one winter, to obtain it whilst we were there was another matter, and entailed some undesirable risk, as the Bosch seemed intent on wiping that village off the face of the earth.

Hope I shall not have to resort to Field Post Cards for some time now.

10.11.1916

Dear Mother and Dad

Very pleased to receive your letters and Edith's too. This must answer for all, but please do not treat me in the same way.

You should hear the "grouse" going on now. Not one of us has received a letter tonight. The men are showering considerable displeasure on the unfortunate "Post-Men" detailed to collect letters. This is the <u>event</u> of the day and it is very unusual if one of us does not receive a letter.

We have been having some fairly rough weather lately, although not nearly as bad for us as for those on other parts of the front, but there, we all have our share of the rough and the smooth.

Today has made up for much in the past, for I have been able to admire the sunlight on the trees once more. Not the variety or quantity you see, but trees, not battered stumps. Ash and Willow chiefly, and but a row of them with a fine tangle of rough grass and weeds beneath in rich reds, yellows and quiet greens.

Away in the distance too, I can see large banks of trees in their winter brown colouring. The sun brings out the magpies. I like to see them, so boldly marked and noticeable, bold by nature too, I meet them everywhere, even perching on the parapet of a trench.

Letters are a long time reaching us now, the average time lately about 6 days.

23.11.1916

Dear Mother and Dad,

I am back again with the battalion after having a fairly good time at the school for Snipers and Observers. It has made a change and the work was interesting, but I was there not quite long enough to become a really expert shot, but my job is to train others.

However, I gained a few ideas in the theory of good and useful observation and sniping. How things should be done or done to. But believe me, sniping at a school and sniping in grim earnest are two very different things. The former is much too one sided!!! It was bitterly cold while I was there with some snow.

Are you issued with bread coupons yet? I have not seen a newspaper for quite a long time and I am all behind with news of home affairs since seeing the headline in the Daily Mail on that subject. I hope you will not be served with biscuits in lieu of bread as sometimes occurs here, that would be the limit. If you are, write and tell me and I will give you a few tips on how they can be treated and eaten without damaging your teeth. They are much better now, but some issues were large and hard, impossible to eat in the state as issued and not very attractive when "cooked".

I have too seen the label on the top of open tins of biscuits stating it was some firm's make of Puppy Biscuits. These were edible.

17.12.1916

My dear Mother,

Didn't you gasp when you received my telegram, too late, but never mind I am here and home for Christmas. That's glorious isn't it?

I received orders to report here and remain until I obtain "leave" tomorrow, I hope, but not certain. After that Cadet School and a Commission. Will tell you all about it when I see you.

I have missed your parcel, never mind, the boys will thoroughly enjoy the contents and be grateful to you for it. I am too excited and happy to settle down to anything so prosaic as writing a letter.

Love to all and shall be seeing you soon.

BIBLIOGRAPHY

(RSR: Royal Sussex Regiment; WSCC: West Sussex County Council; WSRO: West Sussex Record Office)

Unpublished sources

PRO WO 339/83413. Ralph Ellis Officer Service Record
UCLCA/SR. Ralph Ellis Registry File, Slade School of Art
WSRO Add. Mss. 1606. Letters from Shippams Employees, George Farndale and Charles Tulett
WSRO Add. Mss. 25001. Ellis, R. *A March with the Infantry by Four-Two Eight* (1947-8)
WSRO Add. Mss. 25002-6. Ellis, R. Five manuscript volumes, (1916-21)
WSRO RSR uncatalogued (Museum Accession 3179). Tulett, C. unpublished memoir

Published sources

(Place of publication is London unless otherwise stated.)

2nd Battalion, The Queen's (Royal West Surrey) Regiment War Diary, http://www.queensroyalsurreys.org.uk/war_diaries/local/2Bn_Queens.shtml.
Blunden, E. 2000. *Undertones of War* (Penguin)
Campbell-Smith, D. 2011. *Masters of the Post: The Authorised History of the Royal Mail* (Allen Lane)
Fussell, Paul. 1975. *The Great War and Modern Memory* (OUP, Oxford)
Godfrey, J.D. 2014. 'Mobilisation and Recruitment' in M. Hayes and E. White (eds), *West Sussex: Remembering 1914-18* (WSCC)
Godfrey, J.D. [n.d.]. *Landscapes of War and Peace: Sussex, the South Downs and the Western Front 1914-18* unpublished masters dissertation, University of Buckingham
Gowler, M., and K. Leslie. 1995. *Ralph Ellis of Arundel, 1885 – 1963* (Chichester, WSCC)
Gowler, M. 1997. *Ralph Ellis: Inn sign painter and designer* (Bognor Regis)
Graves, R. 1960. *Goodbye To All That* (Penguin)
Hynes, S. 1997. *A Soldier's Tale* (Allen Lane, The Penguin Press)
Hynes, S. 1990. *A War Imagined* (The Bodley Head)
Lewis-Stempel, J. 2006. *Where Poppies Blow* (Weidenfeld & Nicholson)
— —. 2010. *Six Weeks* (Weidenfeld & Nicholson)
Margary, I. [n.d.]. *Some Experiences of the Great War Whilst Serving with the 7th Battalion Royal Sussex Regiment in France, 1919* original and typescript version in the library of the Sussex Archaeological Society, Barbican House, Lewes, East Sussex
Middlebrook, Martin. 2016. *The First Day on the Somme: 1 July 1916* (Penguin)

Readman, A. 2014. 'The Royal Sussex Regiment' in M. Hayes and E. White (eds) *West Sussex: Remembering 1914-18* (WSCC)

Royal Sussex Regiment. *7th Battalion War Diary May 1915-June 1919* WSRO RSR/MSS/7/11 http://www2.westsussex.gov.uk/learning-resources/LR/7th_battalion_rsr_war_diary_1915-19_rsr_ms_7-11e54c.pdf?docid=740b5720-bbc0-4acc-911a-ea32a1fe95ac&version=-1.

Rutter, O. (ed). [n.d.]. *History of the Seventh (Service) Battalion, The Royal Sussex Regiment*

Sansom, A.J. 1921. *Letters from France: June 1915-July 1917*

Sassoon, S. 1972. *The Complete Memoirs of George Sherston* (Faber and Faber)

Sheffield, Garry. 2003. *The Somme: A New History* (Cassell)

Simkins, P. 1988. *Kitchener's Army* (Manchester)

Winter, D. 1979. *Death's Men* (Penguin)

INDEX

Names of places have been normalised from Ralph Ellis's occasionally erratic spelling, and given where appropriate in their contemporary French form.

Names of persons have been consolidated where possible.

2nd Eastern General Hospital Brighton 237
Achicourt 177, 187, 190
Agny 170, 174, 178, 181, 184, 187, 188, 190, 206, 208, 210, 214, 218
Albert 120, 167, 222
Aldershot 15, 25, 26
Alfred (private) 220
Allouagne 146, 148
Amiens 120, 160
Ancre (river) 222
Annequin 117, 134
Armentières 33, 34, 35, 36, 48, 66, 67, 81, 222
Arran, Isle of 225
Arras 33, 181, 184, 187, 212, 221, 222, 244
Artois 71
Arundel 1, 4, 10, 11, 251, 252, 253, 264
Auchans Castle, Ayrshire 225, 227
Aveluy 166, 175, 222
Balchin (?) 270
Bapaume 187, 211, 212, 244
Beaurains 187
Berles-au-Bois 246, 247
Bernafay 209
Bernafay Wood 182, 183, 196
Bethune 73, 76, 82, 90, 107, 115, 134, 140, 144
Bienvillers-au-Bois 234
Blendecques 16, 29, 30
Blunden, Edmund 8
Bognor Regis 11, 12
Boulogne 15, 28
Bouzincourt 169, 222
Bridger (unknown) 205

Brittain, Vera 3
Brooke, Rupert 3
Bullecourt 185, 231, 239, 240, 243, 247
Bully Grenay 120
Bully-Grenay 155
Bus-lès Artois 163, 168
Butcher (?) 264
Cambrai 102, 222
Champagne 71
Cheeseman (?) 164, 207, 263
Chichester 222
Christmas (1916) 221
Christmas (1917) 222
Christmas 1915 91, 95
Churchill, Maj Winston 87, 88, 267
Cité St Elie 112
Coghill, Sgt 228
Colchester 19, 20
Courcelles 185, 231, 233
Craters, Battle of 118
Croisilles 241
Dainville 172
Dearling (?) 264
Dorking 25
Douvrin 120, 123, 128, 157
Dover 24, 249
Edmeads Farm 59
Ellis, Catherine 11
Ellis, David 251
Ellis, Edith 11, 255
Ellis, Emma 11
Ellis, Frederick 11
Ellis, Gertrude 11, 250, 252, 255
Ellis, Jack 11
Ellis, Jane 11
Ellis, Margaret 251

Ellis, Ralph: A March with the Infantry 2, 7, 252
Ellis, Samuel 11
Ellis, William Benner 11, 250
Épehy 222
Ervillers 244
Essars 234
Estrée-Blanche 152, 154, 156
Étaples 185, 231
Farndale, George 7
Festubert 74, 92, 93, 95, 96, 98
Flers 182, 183, 191, 198, 199, 200, 202
Flers-Courcelette 183
Flers-Guedecourt 182
Flesselles 120, 158
Fleurbaix 222
Folkestone 14, 21, 23, 24, 25, 27
Foncquevillers 234
Frelinghien 39, 41, 47, 64, 65
French, General Sir John 64
Fussell, Paul 6
Gailes, Ayrshire 184, 223, 225, 230
General Abercrombie (pub) 251
Givenchy 74, 90, 91, 92, 97
Godfrey, John 4
Gowler, Margaret (Ralph Ellis's daughter) 6, 10, 251, 255
Graves, Robert 8
Grenay 155
Gueudecourt 191, 211
Guildford 25
Ham-en-Artois 74, 99, 100, 101
Hannescamps 234
Hartney Common 14
Hendecourt 185, 239
Hénencourt 7, 121, 166, 168
Henty & Constable 250
Hindenburg Line 185, 239, 247
Hinges 74, 89, 90, 91, 95
Hingette 74
Hohenzollern Redoubt 72, 75, 102, 103, 105, 110, 117, 119, 136, 140, 141

Hooge 66
Houplines 33, 34, 36, 39, 40, 41, 51, 52
Hulluch 72, 78, 79, 80, 82, 102
Hynes, Samuel 3, 4, 7, 8
Hythe Ranges 20
Irvine, Ayrshire 229
Jacobs, Harry 272
Kilmarnock, Ayrshire 230
King's Head (pub) 251
Kitchener, Field Marshal Lord 25
La Bassée 71, 135
La Boisselle 121, 165, 173, 175
La Rouge Croix 87, 88
Lady Evelyn Mason Hospital 249
Lapugnoy 119, 122, 142, 145, 146, 150, 151, 152, 153, 155
Le Touquet 33, 39
Leighton, Roland 4
Les Deux Magots 251
Lillers 87, 150
Longbourne, Lt-Col 231
Loos 36, 71, 77, 78, 82, 102, 107
Lys (river) 40, 49
Mametz 181, 182, 219
Margary, Ivan 8
Maroc 120, 155, 157
Martinpuich 271
Mazingarbe 82, 107, 127
McCrae, John 6
Milham, (unknown) 53
Military Hospital Chichester 249
Monchy 222
Moreuil 222
Morlancourt 222
Morris, 'Rat' 53
Mullet, Sgt 272
Noeux-les-Mines 69, 130
Norfolk, Duke of 11, 13
Noyelles 72, 82, 102, 109, 114, 116, 127, 130, 133
'O Pips' 2, 37

Observation posts 2, 37, 57, 58, 75, 76, 114, 115, 122, 123, 128, 135, 189, 210, 266
Osborne, Lt-Col W. L. 14, 121
Ovillers 120, 121, 166, 168, 175
Passchendaele (battle of) 185
Ploegsteert 39
Pommier Redoubt 181, 193, 194
Pont de Dieppe 39
Pozières 173
Prince of Wales Hospital Marylebone 249
Romanscamp 232
Royal Sussex Regiment, 7th Battalion 1, 3, 6, 7, 8, 9, 13, 14, 15
Rutter, Owen 10
Sailly-Labourse 73, 106, 130, 143, 144
Saint-Léger 237, 238, 241, 242, 244
Sandling 14, 21
Sansom, Col Alfred 8, 184
Sansom, Ivy 8
Sansom, Lt-Col Alfred 121
Sassoon, Siegfried 8
Scott, Maj-Gen A B 121
Seymour, Gertrude Ada (Ralph Ellis's wife) 11, 250, 251
Seymour, Millicent 12
Shippams factory 7
Shorncliffe 14, 21
Sittingbourne 231
Slade School of Art 250
Somain 222
Somme (battlefield) 5, 33, 120, 121, 159, 181, 182, 217, 256, 271
Somme (river) 15, 106
Songhurst, Sgt B H 22
St David (hospital ship) 249
St Eloi 222
St Hilaire 73, 87, 90
St Omer 87
Steenwerck 31, 32, 39
Stroud, Capt 231
tanks 204, 217

Tonks, Prof Henry 250
Transloy, Battle of 182
Tulett, Charles 7, 8
Vadencourt 235, 245
Verdun 159
Vermelles 72, 73, 75, 82, 85, 102, 104, 106, 115, 117, 119, 120, 125, 134, 137, 139, 143, 144, 155
Vignacourt 120, 160
Whittenstall, Lt-Col 53
Ypres (Second battle of) 33
Ypres (Third battle of) 185, 186, 247
Ypres 15